Voltaire

A Sketch of His Life and Works

J. M. Wheeler, G. W. Foote

Alpha Editions

This edition published in 2024

ISBN : 9789364730044

Design and Setting By
Alpha Editions
www.alphaedis.com
Email - info@alphaedis.com

As per information held with us this book is in Public Domain. This book is a reproduction of an important historical work. Alpha Editions uses the best technology to reproduce historical work in the same manner it was first published to preserve its original nature. Any marks or number seen are left intentionally to preserve its true form.

Contents

INTRODUCTION ....- 1 -
PREFACE ....- 2 -
EARLY LIFE..- 3 -
HEGIRA TO ENGLAND..- 6 -
EXAMPLES FROM ENGLAND.....................................- 11 -
AT CIREY ....- 14 -
"CANDIDE" ....- 20 -
THE ENCYCLOPÆDIA ....- 25 -
LAST DAYS..- 38 -
HIS CHARACTER AND SERVICES ....- 45 -
TRIBUTES TO VOLTAIRE ....- 51 -
SELECTIONS FROM VOLTAIRE'S WORKS History ....- 59 -
DETACHED THOUGHTS ....- 68 -

INTRODUCTION

My share in this little book on Voltaire is a very minor one. My old friend and colleague, Mr. J. M. Wheeler, had written the greater part of the following pages before he brought the enterprise to my attention. I went through his copy with him, and assisted him in making some alterations and additions. I also read the printer's proofs, and suggested some further improvements— if I may call them so without egotism. This is all I have done. The credit for all the rest belongs to him. My name is placed on the title-page for two reasons. The first is, that I may now, as on other occasions, be associated with a dear friend and colleague in this tribute to Voltaire. The second is, that whatever influence I possess may be used in helping this volume to the circulation it deserves.

A.

1.   FOOTE.

November, 1891

PREFACE

HE would be a bold person who should attempt to say something entirely new on Voltaire. His life has often been written, and many are the disquisitions on his character and influence. This little book, which at the bicentenary of his birth I offer as a Freethinker's tribute to the memory of the great liberator, has no other pretension than that of being a compilation seeking to display in brief compass something of the man's work and influence. But it has its own point of view. It is as a Freethinker, a reformer, and an apostle of reason and universal toleration that I esteem Voltaire, and I have considered him mainly under this aspect. For the sketch of the salient points of his career I am indebted to many sources, including Condorcet, Duvernet, Desnoisterres, Parton, Espinasse, Collins, and Saintsbury, to whom the reader, desirous of fuller information, is referred. Mr. John Morley's able work and Col. Hamley's sketch may also be recommended.

That we are this year celebrating the bicentenary of Voltaire's birth should remind us of how far our age has advanced from his, and also of how much we owe to our predecessors. The spread of democracy and the advance of science which distinguish our time both owe very-much to the brilliant iconoclasts of the last century, of whom Voltaire was the chief. In judging the work of the laughing sage of France we must remember that in his day the feudal laws still obtained in France, and a man might be clapped in prison for life without any trial. The poor were held to be born into the world for the service of the rich, and it was their duty to be subject to their masters, not only to the good and gentle, but also to the froward. Justice was as easily bought as jewels. The Church was omnipotent and freethought a crime. If Voltaire's influence is no longer what it was, it is because he has altered that. We can no longer keenly feel the evils against which he contended. His work is, however, by no means fully accomplished. While any remnant of superstition, intolerance, and oppression remains, his unremitting warfare against *l'infâme* should be an inspiration to all who are fighting for the liberation and progress of humanity.

Nov. 1894. J. M. WHEELER.

EARLY LIFE

TWO hundred years ago, on November 21st, 1604, a child emerged on the world at Paris. The baptismal register on the following day gave the name François Marie Arouet, and the youth afterwards christened himself Voltaire.(1) The flesh was so weakly that the babe was *ondovc* (the term employed for informal sprinkling with water at home), lest there might be no time for the ecclesiastical rite.

1. He was a younger son. The name Voltaire is, perhaps, an anagram of the Arouet 1. j. (le jeune) the u being converted into r, and the j into r. In like manner, an old college- tutor of his, Père Thoulié, transformed himself, by a similar anagrammatic process, into the Abbé Olivet— omitting the unnecessary h from his original name. This method of reforming a plebeian name into one more distinguished-looking seems not to have been uncommon in those times, as Jean Baptiste Pocquelin took the name of Molière, and Charles Secondât that of Montesquieu.

Something may have been wrong with the performance of the sacred ceremony, since the child certainly grew up to think more of "the world, the flesh, and the devil" than of the other trinity of Father, Son, and Holy Ghost. His father was a respectable attorney, and his mother came of noble family. His godfather and early preceptor was the Abbé de Chateauneuf, who made no pietist of him, but introduced him to his friend, the famous Ninon l'Enclos, the antiquated Aspasia who is said to have inspired a passion in the l'Abbé Gedouin at the age of eighty, and who was sufficiently struck with young Voltaire to leave him a legacy of two thousand francs, wherewith to provide himself a library.

Voltaire showed when quite a child an unsurpassed facility for verse-making. He was educated at a Jesuit college, and the followers of Jesus have ever since reproached him with Jesuitism. Possibly he did imbibe some of their "policy" in the propaganda of his ideas. Certainly he saw sufficient of the hypocrisy and immorality of religious professors to disgust him with the black business, and he said in after-life that the Jesuits had taught him nothing worth learning.

He learnt a certain amount of Latin and a parcel of stupidities. But, indifferent as this education was, it served to encourage his already marked literary tendency. Voltaire is said to have told his father when he left college, at the age of fifteen, "I wish to be a man of letters, and nothing else." "That," M. Arouet is reported to have replied, "is the profession of a man who wishes to be a burden to his family and to die of starvation." He would have no such nonsense. Francois must study law; and to Paris he went with that intent. For three years he was supposed to do so, but he bestowed more attention on the gay society of the Temple, to which his godfather introduced him, "the most amusing fellow in the world," and which was presided over by the Abbé de Chaulieu. The time which he was compelled to spend in law studies, and at the desk of a *procureur*, was by no means lost to his future fortunes, whether in the pursuit of fame or wealth. During that hated apprenticeship he doubtless caught up some knowledge of law and business, which stood him in good stead in after years. He tells us that his father thought him lost, because he mixed with good society and wrote verses. For these he got sufficient reputation to be first exiled to Tulle, then to Sully, and finally thrown into the Bastille on suspicion of having written lampoons on the government. The current story tells how the Regent, walking one day in the Palais Royal, met Voltaire, and accosted him by offering to bet that he would show him what he had never seen before. "What is that?" asked Voltaire. "The Bastille." "Ah, monseigneur! I will take the Bastille as seen." On the next morning, in May, 1717, Voltaire was arrested in his bedroom and lodged in the Bastille.

After nearly a year's imprisonment, during which he gave the finishing touches to his tragedy of *Œdipus*, and sketched the epic *Henriade*, in which he depicts the massacre of Bartholomew, the horrors of religious bigotry, and the triumph of toleration under Henry IV., he was released and conducted to the Regent. While Voltaire awaited audience there was a thunderstorm. "Things could not go on worse," he said aloud, "if there was a Regency above." His conductor, introducing him to the Regent, said, repeating the remark, "I bring you a young man whom your Highness has just released from the Bastille, and whom you should send back again." The Regent laughed, and promised, if he behaved well, to provide for him. "I thank your Highness for taking charge of my board," returned Voltaire, "but I beseech you not to trouble yourself any more about my lodging."

In his first play, *Œdipe*, appeared the celebrated couplet:

"Nos prêtres ne sont pas ce qu'un vain peuple pense!

Notre crédulité fait toute leur science." (1)

1. "Our priests are not what foolish people suppose; all their science is derived from our credulity."

These lines were afterwards noted by Condorcet as "the first signal of a war, which not even the death of Voltaire could extinguish." It was at this period that he first took the name of Arouet de Voltaire. He produced two more tragedies, *Artemire* and *Mariamne*; a comedy, *The Babbler*; and prepared his world-famous *Henriade*. A portrait, painted by Largillière at about this period, has often been engraved. It exhibits a handsome young gentleman, full of grace and spirit, with a smiling mouth, animated eyes, intellectual forehead, and a fine hand in a fine ruffle.

HEGIRA TO ENGLAND

THE story of how Voltaire came to England is worth the telling, as it illustrates the condition of things in France in the early part of last century. Voltaire left France for England, which his acquaintance with Lord Bolingbroke induced him to desire to visit. It was his Hegira, whence he returned a full-fledged Prophet of the French. He went a poet, he returned a philosopher. Dining at the Duke of Sully's table he presumed to differ from the Chevalier de Rohan—Chabot, a relative of Cardinal Rohan. The aristocrat asked, "Who is that young fellow who talks so loudly?" "Monsieur le Chevalier," replied Voltaire, "it is a man who does not bear a great name but who knows how to honor the name he does bear."(1) It was insufferable that the son of a bourgeois should thus speak his mind to a Rohan. A few days afterwards, when again dining with the Duke, he was called out by a false message, and seized and caned by ruffians until a voice cried "Enough." That word was a fresh blow, for the young poet recognised the voice of the Chevalier. He returned to the Duke and asked him to assist in obtaining redress. His grace shrugged his shoulders and took no further notice of this insult to his guest. Voltaire never visited the Duke again, and, it is said, erased his ancestor's name from the *Henriade*. He was equally unsuccessful in seeking redress from the Regent. "You are a poet, and you have had a good thrashing; what can be more natural?" He retired, to study English and fencing; and reappeared with a challenge to the Chevalier, who accepted it, but informed his relations. It was against the law for a commoner to challenge a nobleman. Next morning, instead of meeting de Rohan, he met officers armed with a *lettre de cachet* consigning him to the Bastille. After nearly a month's incarceration he was liberated on condition that he left the country. Having no wish to spend a second year in prison, he had himself applied for permission to visit England. Voltaire felt keenly the indignity to which he had been subjected. In a letter of instruction written from England to his agent he says: "If my debtors profit by my misfortune and absence to refuse payment, you must not trouble to bring them to reason: 'tis but a trifle." Yet a book has been written on Voltaire's avarice.

1. Some of the accounts say that Voltaire said, "You, my lord, are the last of your house; I am the first of mine."

Voltaire was conducted to Calais and arrived in England on Whit-Monday, 1726. He landed near Greenwich and witnessed the Fair. All seemed bright. The park and river were full of animation. Here there was no Bastille, no fear of the persecution of the great or the spies of the police. He had excellent introductions. Bolingbroke he had met in exile at La Source in 1721, and he had learnt to regard the illustrious Englishman who possessed "all the learning of his country and all the politeness of ours." Voltaire, like Pope, may be said to have been, at any rate for a time, an eager disciple of the exiled English statesman. Now Voltaire was the exile; Bolingbroke, for a while, the host, at Dawley, near Uxbridge. But he had other English friends, notably Mr. (afterwards Sir Everard) Falkener, an English merchant trading in the Levant, from whose house at Wandsworth most of his letters are dated. For Sir Everard, Voltaire always retained the warmest feelings of friendship, and forty years later returned hospitality to his sons.

Voltaire spent two years and eight months in England, living during part of the time in Maiden Lane, Covent Garden, and during another part at Wandsworth. This visit was probably the most important event in his life. It was here he lit the torch of Freethought with which he fired the continent. Here he mastered the arguments of the English deists, Bolingbroke, Toland, Tindal, Shaftesbury, Chubb, Collins, and Woolston, which he afterwards used with such effect. Here he saw the benefits of parliamentary government. Here he imbibed the philosophy of Locke and the science of Newton. Indeed it may be said there is hardly one of Voltaire's important works but bears traces of his visit to our country. Yet of this momentous epoch of his life the records are scanty. When he grew famous every letter and anecdote was preserved, but in 1727 Voltaire was but a young man of promise. Carlyle, in the tenth book of his *Frederick the Great*, says: "But mere inanity and darkness visible reign in all his Biographies over this period of his life, which was above all others worth investigating." Messrs. J. C. Collins and A. Ballantyne have since done much to elucidate this noteworthy period.

Pope was one of the persons Voltaire desired to see. He had already described him as "the most elegant, most correct, and most harmonious poet they ever had in England." Pope could only speak French with difficulty, and Voltaire could not make himself understood. The result being unsatisfactory, Voltaire did not seek further company until he had acquired the language. An anecdote in Chetworth's *History of the Stage* relates that he was in the habit of attending the theatre with the play in his hand. By this method he obtained more proficiency in the language in a week than he could otherwise have obtained in a month. Madame de Genlis had the audacity to assert that Voltaire never knew English, yet it is certain he could, before he was many months in this country, both speak and write it with facility. By Nov. 16, 1726, he wrote to Pope, after that poet's accident while driving near Bolingbroke's estate at Dawley. In writing to his friend Thieriot, in France, he sometimes used English, for the same reason, he said, that Boileau wrote in Latin—not to be understood by too curious people. Voltaire is said to have once found his knowledge of English of practical use. The French were unpopular, and in one of his rambles he was menaced by a mob. He said:

"Brave Englishmen, am I not already unhappy enough in not having been born among you?" His eloquence had such success that, according to Longchamp and Wagnière, the people wished to carry him on their shoulders to his house.

While in this country he wrote in English a portion of his tragedy *Brutus*, inspired by and dedicated to Bolingbroke,

and two essays, one on the Civil Wars of France, and one on Epic Poetry. In the introduction to the essays he expresses his conception of his own position as a man of letters in a foreign country. As these essays, although popular at the time, are now rare, I transcribe a paragraph or two from them:

"The true aim of a relation is to instruct men, not to gratify their malice. We should be busied chiefly in giving a faithful account of all the useful things and extraordinary persons, whom to know, and to imitate, would be a benefit to our country. A traveller who writes in that spirit is a merchant of a nobler kind, who imports into his native country the arts and virtues of other nations."

In his *Essay on Epic Poetry* Voltaire shows he had made a study of Milton, though his criticism can scarcely, be considered an advance upon that of Addison. He displays constant admiration for Tasso, to whom he was perhaps attracted by his sufferings at the hands of an ignoble nobility. He says:

"The taste of the English and of the French, though averse to any machinery grounded upon enchantment, must forgive, nay commend, that of Armida, since it is the source of so many beauties. Besides, she is a Mahometan, and the Christian religion allows us to believe that those infidels are under the immediate influence of the devil." In this essay appears the first mention of the story of Newton and the apple tree.

Voltaire closely studied all branches of English literature. He read Shakespeare, and admired his "genius" while censuring his "irregularity." He was the first to introduce him to his countrymen, though he subsequently sought to lessen what he considered their exorbitantly high opinion. The works of Dryden, Waller, Prior, Congreve, Wycherley, Vanbrugh, Rochester and Addison were all devoured, and he took an especial interest in Butler's witty *Hudibras*. He was acquainted with the popular sermons of Archbishop Tillotson and the speculations of Berkeley. He had read the works of Shaftesbury, Tindal, Chubb, Garth, Mandeville and Woolston.

Voltaire became acquainted with most of the celebrities in England. He visited the witty Congreve, who begged his guest to consider him not as an author but as a gentleman. Voltaire answered with spirit: "If you had the misfortune to be merely a gentleman, I should never have come to see you."

He knew James Thomson of *The Seasons*, and "discovered in him a great genius and a great simplicity." With didactic Young, of the *Night Thoughts*, who glorified God with his "egoism turned heavenward," he formed a friendship which remained unbroken despite their differences of opinion on religion. He pushed among his English friends the subscription list for the *Henriade*, which proved a great success—although King George II. was not fond of "boetry"—reaching three editions in a short period. The money thus obtained formed the foundation of the fortune which Voltaire accumulated, not by his writings, but by his ability in finance. At that time, in France, as our author remarked, "to make the smallest fortune it was better to say four words to the mistress of a king than to write a hundred volumes." His sojourn in England may be said to have secured him both independence of mind and independence of fortune.

What pleased him most in England was liberty of discussion. In the year in which he came over, Elwall was acquitted on a charge of blasphemy, the collected works of Toland were published, and also Collins's *Scheme of Literal Prophecy*, and the First Discourse of Woolston on Miracles. The success of this last work, which boldly applied wit and ridicule to the Gospel narrative, struck him with admiration. In the very month, however, when Voltaire left England (March 1729) Woolston was tried and sentenced to a year's imprisonment and a fine of £100. Voltaire volunteered a third of the sum, but the brave prisoner refused to give an assurance that he would not offend again, and died in prison in 1733. Voltaire always spoke of Woolston with the greatest respect.

Voltaire retained his esteem for England and the English to the last. Oliver Goldsmith relates that he was in his company one evening when one of the party undertook to revile the English language and literature. Diderot defended them, but not brilliantly. Voltaire listened awhile in silence, which was, as Goldsmith remarks, surprising, for it was one of his favorite topics. However, about midnight, "Voltaire appeared at last roused from his reverie. His whole frame seemed animated. He began his defence with the utmost elegance mixed with spirit, and now and then he let fall his finest strokes of raillery upon his antagonist; and his harangue lasted until three in the morning. I must confess that, whether from national partiality or from the elegant sensibility of his manner, I never was more charmed, nor did I ever remember so absolute a victory as he gained in this dispute."

Voltaire corresponded with English friends to the latest period of his life. Among his correspondents were Lord and Lady Bolingbroke, Sir E. Falkener, Swift, Hume, Robertson, Horace Walpole, George Colman and Lord Chatham. We find him asking Falkener to send him the *London Magazine* for the past three years. To the same friend he wrote from Potsdam in 1752, hoping that his *Vindication of Bolingbroke* was translated, as it would annoy the priests, "whom I have hated, hate, and shall hate till doomsday." In the next year, writing from Berlin, he says: "I hope to come over myself, in order to print my true works, and to be buried in the land of freedom. I require no subscription, I desire no benefit. If my works are neatly printed, and cheaply sold, I am satisfied."

To Thieriot he said: "Had I not been obliged to look after my affairs in France, depend upon it I would have spent the rest of my days in London." Long afterwards he wrote to his friend Keate: "Had I not fixed the seat of my retreat in the free corner of Geneva, I would certainly live in the free corner of England; I have been for thirty years the disciple of your ways of thinking." At the age of seventy he translated Shakespeare's *Julius Cæsar*. Mr. Collins says: "The kindness and hospitality which he received he never forgot, and he took every opportunity of repaying it. To be an Englishman was always a certain passport to his courteous consideration." He compared the English to their own beer, "the froth atop, dregs at bottom, but the bulk excellent." When Martin Sherlock visited him at Ferney in 1776, he found the old man, then in his eighty-third year, still full of his visit to England. His gardens were laid out in English fashion, his favorite books were the English classics, the subject to which he persistently directed conversation was the English nation.

The memory of Voltaire has been but scurvily treated in the land he loved so well. For over a century, calumny and obloquy were poured upon him. Johnson said of Rousseau: "I would sooner sign a sentence for his transportation than that of any felon who has gone from the Old Bailey these many years." *Boswell*: "Sir, do you think him as bad a man as Voltaire?" *Johnson*: "Why, sir, it is difficult to settle the proportion of iniquity between them." And this represents an opinion which long endured among the religious classes. But it is at length being recognised that, with all his imperfections, which were after all those of the age in which he lived, he devoted his brilliant genius to the cause of truth and the progress of humanity. He made his exile in England an occasion for accumulating those stores of intelligence with which he so successfully combated the prejudices of the past and promulgated the principles of freedom, and justified his being ranked foremost among the liberators of the human mind.

EXAMPLES FROM ENGLAND

SEVERAL incidents combined to direct Voltaire's attention to clericalism as the enemy of progress and humanity. Soon after his return to France, the famous actress, Adrienne Lecouvreur, for whom he had a high esteem, and who had represented the heroines of his plays, died. The clergy of Paris refused her Christian burial because of her profession, and her corpse was put in a ditch in a cattle-field on the banks of the Seine. Voltaire, who regarded the theatre as one of the most potent instruments of culture and civilisation, at once avenged and consecrated her memory in a fine ode, burning with the fire of a deep pathos, in which he takes occasion to contrast the treatment in England of Mrs. Oldfield, the actress, who was buried in Westminster Abbey. Mr. Lecky says: "The man who did more than any other to remove the stigma that rested upon actors was unquestionably Voltaire. There is, indeed, something singularly noble in the untiring zeal with which he directs poetry and eloquence, the keenest wit, and the closest reasoning to the defence of those who had so long been friendless and despised."

When Voltaire published his *Letters on the English Nation* the copies were seized by the Government and the publisher was thrown into the Bastille. The author would have again tasted the discomforts of that abode if he had not had timely warning from his friend D'Argental, and taken refuge in Lorraine, and afterwards on the Rhine, while his book was torn to pieces and burned in Paris by the public executioner, as offensive to religion, good morals, and respect for authority. Voltaire had apparently good reason to apprehend treatment of unusual rigor if he had obeyed the summons to give himself up into custody, as he took good care not to do. "I have a mortal aversion to prison," he wrote to D'Argental. "I am ill; a confined air would have killed me, and I should probably have been thrust into a dungeon."

Voltaire's *Letters on the English* reads at the present day as so mild a production that it is hard to understand its suppression. Yet it was a true instinct which detected that the work was directed against the principle of authority. The introduction of English thought was destined to become an explosive element shattering the feudalism of Europe. There were, moreover, some hard hits at the state of things in France. "The English nation," says Voltaire, "is the only one which has succeeded in restricting the power of kings by resisting it." Again: "How I love the English boldness, how I love men who say what they think!"

Voltaire gives a peculiar reason for the non-appreciation by the English of Molière's *Tartuffe*, the original of Mawworm if not of Uriah Heep. He says they are not pleased with the portrayal of characters they do not know. "One there hardly knows the name of devotee, but they know well that of honest man. One does not see there imbeciles who put their souls into others' hands, nor those petty ambitious men who establish a despotic sway over women formerly wanton and always weak, and over men yet more weak and contemptible." We fancy Voltaire must have seen society mainly as found among the Freethinkers. Could he give so favorable a verdict did he visit us now? The same remark applies to his statement that there was "no privilege of hunting in the grounds of a citizen, who, at the same time, is not permitted to fire a gun in his own field." But this, as well as the more important passage that "no one is exempted from taxation for being a nobleman or priest," was probably intended exclusively for the benefit of his compatriots. He was, however, not without a little touch of ridicule at the incongruities he detected in our countrymen. Thus he notes in one of his letters: "They learn Vanini and translate Lucretius for Monsieur le Dauphin to get by heart, and then, while they deride the polytheism of the ancients, they worship the Congregation of the Saints."

Those educated in the current delusion that Voltaire was a mere mocker will be surprised to find the temperate way in which he speaks of the Quakers. Here, where there was such excellent opportunity for raillery, Voltaire shows he had a genuine admiration for their simplicity of life, the courage of their convictions, their freedom from priestcraft, and their distaste for warfare. In these *Letters,* as in all his writings, he proves how far he was the embodiment of the new era by his boldly expressed preference for industrial over military pursuits.

In his remarks on the Church of England, Voltaire, however, gives an unmistakable touch of his quality: "One cannot have public employment in England or Ireland, without being of the number of faithful Anglicans. This reason, which is an excellent proof, has converted so many Nonconformists that not a twentieth part of the nation is out of the pale of the dominant church."

After alluding to the "holy zeal" of ministers against dissenters, and of the lower House of Convocation, who "from time to time burnt impious books, that is, books against themselves," he says: "When they learn that, in France, young fellows noted only for debauchery and raised to the prelacy by female intrigue, openly pursue their amours, compose love-songs, give every day elaborate delicate suppers, then go to implore the illumination of the Holy Spirit, boldly calling themselves the successors of the Apostles—they thank God they are Protestants. But they are abominable heretics, to be burnt by all the devils, as Master François Rabelais says; and that is why I do not meddle with their affairs."

The Presbyterians fare little better, for Voltaire relates that, when King Charles surrendered to the Scots, they made that unfortunate monarch undergo four sermons a day. To them it is owing that only genteel people play cards on Sunday: "the rest of the nation go either to church, to the tavern, or to see their mistresses."

His admiration for English philosophy was startling to the French mind. Locke's Essay became his philosophical gospel. "For thirty years," he writes in 1768, "I have been persecuted by a crowd of fanatics because I said that Locke is the Hercules of Metaphysics, who has fixed the boundaries of the human mind."

AT CIREY

A COMMON admiration for Locke and Newton cemented his attachment to the Marquise du Châtelet, a lady distinguished from others of her age by her love of the sciences. With her Voltaire lived for over fifteen years at the Chateau of Cirey, in Campagne, "far from the madding crowd's ignoble strife," and, as Voltaire phrased it, "nine miles from a lemon." Voltaire was at the outset forty and Madame twenty-seven, neither handsome nor well-formed, yet pleasing. She united learning with a zest for pleasure, and with the handsome fortune which Voltaire brought to the establishment was enabled to satisfy both tastes. Life at Cirey was varied by jaunts to Paris, Brussels and Sceaux, at which last place he wrote *Zadig*, one of his lightest and most characteristic burlesque stories.

Madame du Châtelet has been much laughed at; but in the days when ladies take prizes in mathematics, that should be a thing of the past. Hard intellectual labor rather than the pursuit of pleasure characterised life at Cirey, or rather its inmates found their pleasure in their work. Madame would be translating Newton or studying Leibnitz. Her mathematical tutor worked at physical science in a gallery which had been built expressly for him. Voltaire would be aiding each in turn, or, ever faithful to his first love the drama, occupied with the writing or production of a tragedy or comedy for the theatre also attached to the premises. His production was as ever incessant. At the time of his first settlement there, Pope's *Essay on Man* had been published. It suggested a *Discourse on Man*, in which he sought not to justify the ways of God to man, but to make man contented with his lot, not vainly inquiring into the why and wherefore of things. With Madame he wrote *Elements of the Newtonian Philosophy*, a work highly praised by Lord Brougham, who says: "The power of explaining an abstract subject in easy and accurate language, language not in any way beneath the dignity of science, though quite suited to the comprehension of uninformed persons, is unquestionably shown in a manner which only makes it a matter of regret that the singularly gifted author did not carry his torch into all the recesses of natural philosophy." The French Government, despite the influence of aristocratic friends, refused to print a work opposed to the system of Descartes, and the volume had to be printed in Holland. For Madame, who despised the "old almanack" histories then current, in place of which Voltaire aimed at producing something more profitable to the readers, he wrote his *Essay on the Manners and Spirit of Nations*, in which for the first time in modern literature he applied philosophy to the teaching of history. He dissipated the dull dreams and deceits of the monks, and fixed attention on the real condition of things. With Voltaire, the commonest invention which improves the human lot is of more importance than battles and sieges. He gives importance to the physical and intellectual improvement of man. Brougham remarks that Voltaire's Philosophy of History was written as a prelude to the Essay on the Spirit of Nations, but the whole work deserves that title. Buckle classes him with Bolingbroke and Montesquieu, the fathers of modern history, and all sceptics; and even now, says Lecky, no historian can read him without profit. Other contributions to history were the *History of Charles XII.*, a masterpiece of vivid and vigorous narrative, and *The Age of Louis XIV*. It was here he wrote his too famous *Pucelle*, which he afterwards described as "piggery," as well as some of the most famous of his plays, including. *Ilzire, Zuline, L'Enfant Prodigue, Mahomet and Mérope*, the best of his tragedies. With that impish spirit in which he ever delighted, he induced the Pope to accept the dedication of his play of *Mahomet*, and then laughed at his infallible Holiness for being unable to see that the shafts supposed to be directed at the impostor of Arabia were really aimed at fanaticism in another quarter.

To his first and last love, the French theatre, Voltaire contributed nearly sixty pieces, the majority of which are tragedies. *Zaire* and *Mérope* suffice to show the excellence he obtained in the classic drama. The first-named was written in three weeks, a wonderful *tour de force*. *Olympic*—written in old age—occupied but six days, though in this we must agree with the friend who told the author that he should not have rested on the seventh day. Voltaire's plays indeed contain occasional fine passages, but they have not the rich delineation of character necessary for works of the first rank. It has been well remarked that in his dramas, as in history, he sought to portray not so much individuals as epochs. In *Mahomet* his subject is a great fanaticism; in *Alzire*, the conquest of America; in *Brutus*, the formation of the Roman power; in the *Death of Cæsar*, the rise of the empire or the ruin of that power. It is noteworthy that, despite his excess of comic talent, Voltaire preferred to devote his mind to tragedy rather than to comedy, in which one might have fancied he would have excelled. In truth, his desire to support the dignity of the stage stood in the way of his shining in comedy. Voltaire also at this period wrote a *Life of Molière*, in which he mingled criticism with biography.

Madame de Grafigny, who visited at Cirey, says he was so greedy of his time, so intent upon his work, that it was sometimes necessary to tear him from his desk for supper. "But when at table, he always has something to tell, very facetious, very odd, very droll, which would often not sound well except in his mouth, and which shows him still as he has painted himself for us—

Toujours un pied dans le cercueil,

De l'autre faisant des gambades."(1)

1.   Ever one foot in the grave,
And gambolling with the other.

"To be seated beside him at supper, how delightful!" she adds. Voltaire at Cirey was out of harm's way, and could and did devote himself to his natural bent in literary work. Madame du Châtelet was sometimes "gey ill to live with." but she preserved him from many annoyances and helped him somewhat at Court. Thanks to the Duc de Richelieu, his patron and debtor, he was appointed historiographer-royal in 1745, with a salary of two thousand livres attached, and in the following year was elected one of the Forty of the French Academy.

His life with Madame du Châtelet had shown him the possibility of woman being man's intellectual companion. With what scorn does he make a lady, who claims equal rights in the matter of divorce with her husband, say:

"My husband replies that he is my head and my superior, that he is taller than me by more than an inch, that he is hairy as a bear, and that, consequently, I owe him everything and that he owes me nothing." This was long before woman's rights were thought of.

Voltaire and Frederick the Great.

While still at Cirey, Voltaire received many a flattering invitation from the Prince Royal of Prussia. Their correspondence, in the words of Carlyle, "sparkles notably with epistolary grace and vivacity," though now mainly interesting as an illustration of two memorable characters and of their century. Voltaire helped him with his *Anti-Machiavelli*, remarking afterwards that had Machiavelli had a prince for a pupil, the very first thing he would have advised him to do would have been so to write. Frederick was bent on having the personal acquaintance and attendance of the renowned poet and philosopher. Much incense and mutual admiration passed, and at length, when he ascended the throne, Voltaire paid him several visits. On one occasion it was a diplomatic one, to cement a union between France and Prussia. Macaulay sneers at this "childish craving for political distinction," and Frederick remarks that he brought no credentials with him. The correspondence and mutual admiration continued. Carlyle characteristically says: "Admiration sincere on both sides, most so on the Prince's, and extravagantly expressed on both sides, most so on Voltaire's." In one of his letters, Frederick says "there can be in nature but one God and one Voltaire." If Voltaire was more extravagant than this, at least the paint was laid on more delicately. Frederick's flattery, indeed, was not very carefully done. Thus, in writing to Voltaire he says: "You are like the white elephant for which the King of Persia and the Great Mogul make war; and the possession of which forms one of their titles. If you come here you will see at the head of mine, 'Frederick by the Grace of God, King of Prussia, Elector of Brandenburg, Possessor of Voltaire, &c., &c.'" But the Marquise du Châtelet considered that no King should displace a lady. She loved him; *"jamais pour deux"* she says; and perhaps, at the bottom of her heart, regretted the reputation which must have been ever a rival. At her death, Frederick renewed his invitation, expressing himself as now "one of your oldest friends," and Voltaire, cut loose from his moorings, submitted to be tempted to the atmosphere of a court which he had before found little suited to a lover of truth, justice, and liberty.

The first of these visits, in September 1740, is thus satirically described by Voltaire: "I was conducted into his majesty's apartment, in which I found nothing but four bare walls. By the light of a wax candle I perceived a small truckle bed, two feet and a half wide, in a closet, upon which lay a little man, wrapped up in a morning gown of blue cloth. It was his majesty, who lay sweating and shaking, beneath a beggarly coverlet, in a violent ague fit. I made my bow, and began my acquaintance by feeling his pulse, as if I had been his first physician. The fit left him, and he rose, dressed himself, and sat down to table with Algarotti, Keizerling, Maupertuis, the ambassador to the states-general, and myself; where, at supper, we treated most profoundly on the immortality of the soul, natural liberty, and the *Androgynes* of Plato." Frederick says, in a letter to Jordan, dated September 24th: "I have at length seen Voltaire, whom I was so anxious to become acquainted with; but, alas! I saw him when I was under the influence of my fever, and when my mind and my body were equally languid. Now, with persons like him, one must not be ill; on the contrary, one must be very well, and even, if possible, in better health than usual. He has the eloquence of Cicero, the mildness of Pliny, and the wisdom of Agrippa: he unites, in a word, all that is desirable of the virtues and talents of three of the greatest men of antiquity. His intellect is always at work; and every drop of ink that falls from his pen, is transformed at once into wit. He declaimed to us *Mahomet*, an admirable tragedy he has composed, which transported us with delight: for myself, I could only admire in silence."

The intercourse and disruption of the friendship between Voltaire and Frederick—"the two original men of their century," as Carlyle calls them—has been inimitably told by that great writer whose temperament and training enabled him to do so much justice to the one and so little to the other. Voltaire must be excused for wishing to lead the King in the path of reason and enlightened toleration to peace. But the Court of Potsdam was in truth no place for him, and the Frenchmen not unnaturally regarded him as a deserter. Macaulay says: "We have no hesitation in saying that the poorest author of that time in London, sleeping in a hulk, dining in a cellar with a cravat of paper and a skewer for a shirt-pin, was a happier man than any of the literary inmates of Frederick's Court." Voltaire's position was sure to excite jealousy, and his scathing wit was bound to get him in trouble. He could touch up the King's French verses for a consideration, but could not be kept from laughing at his poetry. "I have here a bundle of the King's dirty linen to bleach," he said once, pointing to the MSS. sent to him for correction; and the bearers of course conveyed the sarcasm to his Majesty. On the other side Voltaire heard from Julien Offray de la Mettrie, author of *Man a Machine*, whom Voltaire called the most frank atheist in Europe, that the King had said: "I still want Voltaire for another year—one sucks the orange before throwing away the skin." That orange-skin stuck in Voltaire's throat, and when atheist La Mettrie died 11th November,

1751, from eating a pie supposed to be of pheasant but in reality of eagle and pork, Voltaire observes: "I should have liked to put to La Mettrie, in the article of death, fresh inquiries about the orange-skin. That fine soul, on the point of quitting the world, would not have dared to-lie. There is much reason to suppose that he spoke the truth." Voltaire could neither submit to the domination of the Court coterie nor to that of their master. He offended Frederick, not so much by writing as by publishing his merciless ridicule of Maupertuis, the President of the Berlin Academy of Sciences—an institution suggested by Voltaire, who had indeed recommended Maupertuis as President—in his inimitable *Diatribe of Doctor Akakia, Physician to the Pope*, which Macaulay says, even at this time of day, it is not easy for any person who has the least perception of the ridiculous to read without laughing till he cries. But a public insult to the President of his Academy was an insult to the King, and the work was publicly burnt and Voltaire placed under arrest. But the matter blew over, though Voltaire sent back his cross and key of office, which the King returned. Voltaire wisely tried to rid himself of the intolerable constraint, and made ill-health the pretext of flight, going first to Plombières to take the waters. But he could not resist sending another shot at poor Maupertuis; and the King, perhaps considering he had forfeited claim to consideration, resolved to punish him. At Frankfort, nominally a free city but really dominated by a Prussian resident, he was arrested, together with his niece Madame Denis, and detained in an inn, even after he had given up his gold key as chamberlain, his cross and ribbon of the Order of Merit, and his copy of a privately printed volume of the royal rhymester's poetry, for which he was ordered to be arrested. The volume was evidently the most important article in such mischievous hands, especially as it was said to contain satires on reigning potentates. Voltaire had left it at Leipsic, and had to wait, guarded by soldiers, till it arrived, and also till the King's permission was accorded him to pass on to France. Voltaire relieved his rage by composing what he called *Memoirs of the Life of M. de Voltaire*, in which all the king's faults and foibles, real and imaginary, as well as his literary pretensions, were unsparingly ridiculed. Frederick forgave Voltaire for having been ill-used by him, and some time after took the first step in reconciliation by sending him back the volume of poems. An amicable correspondence was renewed, though probably each felt they were better at a distance. Voltaire, even while he kept in his desk this libellous *Life* which perhaps he never, intended to publish, was generous and far-sighted enough to seek to make peace between Prussia and France at a time when Frederick was at the lowest ebb of his fortunes; while Frederick was great enough to permit the free circulation of the libel in Berlin. Morley says: "To have really contributed in the humblest degree, for instance, to a peace between Prussia and her enemies, in 1759, would have been an immeasurably greater performance for mankind than any given book which Voltaire could have written. And, what is still better worth observing, Voltaire's books would not have been the powers they were but for this constant desire in him to come into the closest contact with the practical affairs of the world." "What sovereign in Europe do you fear the most?" was once asked of Frederick, who frankly replied *"Le roi Voltaire,"* for here he knew was a potentate whose kingdom had no bounds, and who would transmit his influence to posterity. Frederick lived to pronounce a panegyric upon him before the Berlin Academy, in the year of his death. "The renown of Voltaire," he predicted, "will grow from age to age, transmitting his name to immortality."

"CANDIDE"

AFTER this disastrous termination of court life Voltaire determined to try complete independence. Permission to establish himself in France being refused, he purchased an estate near Geneva. His residence here brought him into correspondence, at first amicable, with the most famous of her citizens, Jean Jacques Rousseau. There was a natural incompatibility of temper which speedily led to a quarrel. Both were sensitive, and Rousseau could not bear even kindly-meant banter. On Rousseau's *Social Contract* Voltaire said it so convinced him of the beauty of man in a state of nature that, after reading it, he ran round me room on all fours. His reply to Rousseau's rebuke for his pessimist poem on the earthquake of Lisbon was the immortal *Candide*, and Rousseau's revenge was to say, slightingly, that he had not read it. When Rousseau thought fit to include Voltaire in the imaginary machinations against him, with which he absurdly changed Hume, Voltaire wrote to D'Alembert: "I have nothing to reproach myself with, save having thought and spoken too well of him."

Voltaire at first seems to have been captivated by the doctrine of Pope's *Essay on Man*. He, however, afterwards wrote: "Those who exclaim that all is well are charlatans. Shaftesbury, who first made the fable fashionable, was a very unhappy man. I have seen Bolingbroke a prey to vexation and rage, and Pope, whom he induced to put this sorry jest into verse, was as much to be pitied as any man I have ever known, misshapen in body, dissatisfied in mind, always ill, always a burden to himself, and harassed by a hundred enemies to his very last moment. Give me, at least, the names of some happy men who will tell me 'All is well.'" His optimism got injured during his journey through life, and was completely shattered by the earthquake at Lisbon in 1755. On this subject he produced a grave poem, notable for its confession of the difficult reconciling the evil of the world with the Beneficence of God? The same subject was dealt with in grotesque fashion in *Candide*, one of the wisest as well as one of the wittiest of works. A philosophy was never more triumphantly reasoned and ridiculed out of court than is optimism in *Candide*. Incident crowds on incident, argument jostles satire, illustration succeeds raillery, all to show the miseries of existence disprove this being the best of all possible worlds. At one moment we are forced to tears at contemplating the atrocities of inhumanity; the next we are forced to laugh at its absurdities. Prudes may be shocked at some incidents. Voltaire said he was not born to sing the praises of saints. He was himself no saint, but rather one of those sinners who had done the world more good than all its saints. But the influence of the work is profoundly good. It is purely humanitarian, War, persecution for religion, slavery, torture, and all forms of cruelty are made hateful by a recital of their facts; and all this is done in so charming, even flippant a manner, that we are laughing all the while we are most profoundly moved. Schopenhauer and Hartmann both enjoyed life, while Voltaire was an invalid most of his days; but they never threw into their pessimism the gaiety of *Candide*. And his peculiarity is, that he makes all man's lower instincts ridiculous as well as detestable.

This character appears in all his work, but, as a fantastic tale, *Candide* stands alone. It brings out Voltaire's most characteristic qualities: his keen eye for whimsicalities and weaknesses; his abhorrence of cruelty and iniquity in high places; his contempt for shams and absence of all veneration for the majesty of nonsensical custom. For mordant satire it is surpassed by *Gulliver's Travels*. But it is briefer; the touch is lighter, and instinct not with morose misanthropy, but hearty philanthropy. The characters are gross caricatures. Was there ever so preposterous an absurdity as Dr. Pangloss? And the incidents are improbable. Was ever so luckless a hero as Candide? What a succession of misfortunes! Candide travels the world in search of his lost beloved Cunégonde, meeting war, the Inquisition, torture, shipwreck, piracy, and slavery, with all their attendant horrors. Even the earthquake of Lisbon is brought in; yet with whimsical pertinacity, Pangloss clings to his flimsy philosophy.

When he re-meets Candide, who had left his tutor as dead, he thus relates his adventures: "But," my dear Pangloss, "how happens it that I see you again?" said Candide. "It is true," answered Pangloss, "you saw me hanged; I ought properly to have been burnt; but, you remember, it rained in torrents when they were going to roast me. The storm was so violent they despaired of kindling the fire; so I was hanged, because they could do no better. A surgeon bought my body, carried it home, and dissected me. He made first a crucial incision from the navel to the neck. One could not have been more badly hanged than I. The executioner of the Holy Inquisition was a sub-deacon, and truly burnt people capitally, but, as for hanging, he was a novice; the cord was wet, and not slipping properly, the noose did not join—in short, I still continued to breathe. The crucial incision made me shriek so that my surgeon fell back, and, imagining it was the devil he was dissecting, ran away in mortal fear, tumbling downstairs in his fright. His wife, hearing the noise, flew from the next room, and saw me stretched upon the table with my crucial incision. Still more terrified than her husband, she ran down also, and fell upon him. When they had a little recovered themselves, I heard her say to the surgeon, 'My dear, how could you think of dissecting a heretic? Don't you know that the devil is always in them? I'll run directly to a priest, to come and exorcise the evil spirit.' I trembled from head to foot at hearing her talk in this manner, and exerted what little strength I had left to cry out, 'Have pity on me!' At length, the Portuguese barber took courage, sewed up my wound, and his wife even nursed me. I was upon my legs in about a fortnight. The barber got me a place as lacquey to a Knight of Malta, who was going to Venice; but finding my master had no money to pay me my wages, I entered into the service of a Venetian merchant, and went with him to Constantinople. One day I took the fancy to enter a mosque, where I saw no one but an old Iman and a very pretty young female devotee, who was saying her prayers. Her neck was quite bare, and in her bosom she had a fine nosegay of tulips, roses, anemones, ranunculuses, hyacinths, and auriculas. She let fall her bouquet. I ran to take it up, and presented it to her with a bow. I was so long in replacing it, that the Iman began to be angry, and, perceiving I was a Christian, he cried out for help. They took me before the Cadi, who ordered me to receive one hundred bastinadoes, and sent me to the galleys. We were continually whipt, and received twenty lashes a day, when the concatenation of sublunary events brought you on board our galley to ransom us from slavery."

"Well, my dear Pangloss," said Candide to him, "now you have been hanged, dissected, whipped, and tugging at the oar, do you continue to think that everything in this world happens for the best?" "I have always abided by my first opinion," replied Pangloss; "for, after all, I am a philosopher; it would not become me to retract. Leibnitz could not be wrong, and 'pre-established harmony' is, besides, the finest thing in the world, as well as a 'plenum' and the 'materia subtilis'."

When Cunégonde is at last found, she is no longer beautiful—but sunburnt, blear-eyed, haggard, withered, and scrofulous. Though ready to fulfil his promise, her brother, a baron whom Candide has rescued from slavery, declares that sister of his shall never marry a person of less rank than a baron. The book is a mass of seeming extravagance, with a deep vein of gold beneath. All flows so smoothly, the reader fancies such fantastic nonsense could not only be easily written, but easily improved. Yet when he notices how every sally and absurdity adds to the effect, how every lightest touch tells, he sees that only the most consummate wit and genius could thus deftly dissect a philosophy of the universe for the amusement of the multitude.

Voltaire tried to save England from the judicial murder of Admiral Byng, who was sacrificed to national pride and political faction in 1757, yet how lightly he touches the history in a sentence: "Dans ce pays ci il est bon de tuer de temps en temps un amiral pour encourager les autres." The pride, pomp, and circumstance of glorious war had no charms for Voltaire. He shows it in its true colors as multitudinous murder and rapine. Religious intolerance and hypocrisy, court domination and intrigue, the evils attendant on idlers, soldiers and priests, are all sketched in lightest outline, and the reader of this fantastic story finds he has traversed the history of last century, seen it at its worst, and seen, too, the forces that tended to make it better, and is ready to exclaim: Would we had another Voltaire now!

The philosophy of *Candide* is that of Secularism. The world as we find it abounds in misery and suffering. If any being is responsible for it, his benevolence can only be vindicated by limiting his power, or his power credited by limiting his goodness. Our part is simply to make the best of things and improve this world here and now. "Work, then, without disputing; it is the only way to render life supportable."

Carlyle did much to impair the influence of Voltaire in England. Yet what is Carlyle's essential doctrine but "Do the work nearest hand," and what is this but a translation of the conclusion of *Candide*: "Il faut cultiver nôtre jardin"?

Those who forget how far more true it is that man is an irrational animal than that he is a rational one, may wonder how Voltaire, having in *Candide* sapped the foundations of belief in an all-good God by a portrayal of the evils afflicting mankind, could yet remain a Theist. The truth seems to be that Voltaire had neither taste nor talents for metaphysics. In the *Ignorant Philosopher* Voltaire seeks to answer Spinoza, without fully understanding his monistic position. He appears to have remained a dualist or modern Manichean—an opinion which James Mill considered was the only Theistic view consistent with the facts. Writing to D'Alembert on the 15th of August, 1767, Voltaire says: "Give my compliments to the Devil, for it is he who governs the world." It is curious that on the day he was writing these lines, one Napoleon Bonaparte had just entered upon the world.

Voltaire appears to have been satisfied with the design argument as proving a deity, though he considered speculation as to the nature of deity useless. He showed the Positivist spirit in his rejection of metaphysical subtleties. "When," he writes, "we have well disputed over spirit and matter, we end ever by no advance. No philosopher has been able to raise by his own efforts the veil which nature has spread over the first principles of things." Again: "I do not know the *quo modo*, true. I prefer to stop short rather than to lose myself." Also: "Philosophy consists in stopping where physics fail us. I observe the effects of nature, but I confess I know no more than you do about first principles." But a deist he ever remained.

Baron de Gleichen, who visited him in 1757, relates that a young author, at his wits' end for the means of living, knocked one day at the poet's door, and to recommend himself said: "I am an apprentice atheist at your service." Voltaire replied: "I have the honor to be a master deist; but though our trades are opposed, I will give you some supper to-night and some work to-morrow. I wish to avail myself of your arms and not of your head."

He thought both atheism and fanaticism inimical to society; but, said he, "the atheist, in his error, preserves reason, which cuts his claws, while those of the fanatic are sharpened in the incessant madness which afflicts him."

Voltaire seems to have been at bottom agnostic holding on to the narrow ledge of theism and afraid to drop.

He says: "For myself, I am sure of nothing. I believe that there is an intelligence, a creative power, a God. I express an opinion to-day; I doubt of it to-morrow; the day after I repudiate it. All honest philosophers have confessed to me, when they were warmed with wine, that the great Being has not given to them one particle more evidence than to me." He believed in the immortality of the soul, yet expresses himself dubiously, saying to Madame du Deffand that he knew a man who believed that when a bee died it ceased to hum. That man was himself.

On the appearance, however, in 1770 of the Baron d'Holbach's *System of Nature*—in which he was very considerably helped by Diderot—Voltaire took alarm at its openly pronounced atheism. "The book," he wrote,

"has made all the philosophers execrable in the eyes of the King and his court. Through this fatal work philosophy is lost for ever in the eyes of all magistrates and fathers of families." He accordingly took in hand to combat its atheism, which he does in the article *Dieu* in the *Philosophical Dictionary*, and in his *History of Jenni* (Johnny), a lad supposed to be led on a course of vice by atheism and reclaimed to virtue by the design argument. Voltaire's real attitude seems fairly expressed in his celebrated mot: "S'il n'y avait pas un dieu, il fraudrait l'inventer"—"If there was not a God it would be necessary to invent one," which, Morin remarks, was exactly what had been done. Morley says: "It was not the truth of the theistic belief in itself that Voltaire prized, but its supposed utility as an assistant to the police."

THE ENCYCLOPÆDIA

VOLTAIRE was a great stimulator of the French *Encyclopædia*, a work designed to convey to the many the information of the few. Here again the inspiration was English. It was the success of the *Cyclopcedia of Arts and Sciences*, edited by the Freethinker Ephraim Chambers, in 1728, which suggested the yet more famous work carried out by Diderot and D'Alembert, with the assistance of such men as Helvetius, Buffon, Turgot, and Condorcet. Voltaire took an ardent interest in the work, and contributed many important articles. The leading contributors were all Freethinkers, but they were under the necessity of advancing their ideas in a tentative way on account of the vigilant censorship. Voltaire not only wrote for the *Encyclopædia*, but gave valuable hints and suggestions to Diderot and D'Alembert, as well as much sound advice. He cautioned them, for instance, against patriotic bias. "Why," he asks D'Alembert, "do you say that the sciences are more indebted to France than to any other nation? Is it to the French that we are indebted for the quadrant, the fire-engine, the theory of light, inoculation, the seed-sower? *Parbleu!* you are jesting! We have invented only the wheelbarrow."

Voltaire wrote the section on History. The first page contained a Voltairean definition of sacred history which even an ignorant censor could hardly be expected to pass. "Sacred History is a series of operations, divine and miraculous, by which it pleased God formerly to conduct the Jewish nation, and to-day to exercise our faith." The iron hand beneath the velvet glove was too evident for this to pass the censorship. Vexatious delay and the enforced excision of important articles attended the progress of the work.

It was the attempted suppression of *l'Encyclopcedie* which showed Voltaire that the time had come for battle.

In 1757 a new edict was issued, threatening with death any one who wrote, printed, or sold any work attacking religion or the royal authority. The same edict assigned the penalty of the galleys to whoever published writings without legal permit. Within six months advocate Barbier recorded in his diary some terrible sentences. La Martelière, verse-writer, for printing clandestinely Voltaire's *Pucelle* and other "such" works, received nine years in the galleys; eight printers and binders employed in the same printing office, the pillory and three years' banishment. Up to the period of the Revolution nothing could be legally printed in France, and no book could be imported, without Government authorisation. Mr. Lecky says, in his *History of England in the Eighteenth Century*: "During the whole of the reign of Lewis XV. there was scarcely a work of importance which was not burnt or suppressed, while the greater number of the writers who were at this time the special, almost the only, glory of France were imprisoned, banished, or fined." Voltaire determined to render the bigots odious and contemptible, and henceforth waged incessant war, continued to the day of his death. In satire on one of the bigots he issued his *Narrative of the Sickness, Confession, Death and Reappearance of the Jesuit Berthier*, as rich a burlesque as that which Swift had written predicting and describing the death of the astrologer Partridge, in accordance with the prediction. Every sentence is a hit. A priest of a rival order is hastily summoned to confess the dying Jesuit, who is condemned to penance in purgatory for 333,333 years, 3 months, 3 weeks, and 3 days, and then will only be let out if some brother Jesuit be found humble and good enough to be willing to apply all his merits to Father Berthier. Even putting his enemy in purgatory, he only condemned the Jesuit every morning to mix the chocolate of a Jansenist, read aloud at dinner a Provincial Letter, and employ the rest of the day in mending the chemises of the nuns of Port Royal.

From Ferney he poured forth a wasp-swarm of such writings under all sorts of pen-names, and dated from London, Amsterdam, Berne, or Geneva. He had sufficient stimulus in the bigotry, intolerance, and atrocious iniquities perpetrated in the name of religion.

Voltaire, moreover, determined himself to uphold the work of the *Encyclopædia* in more popular form. He put forward first his *Questions upon the Encyclopædia*, in which he deals with some important articles of that work, with others of his own. This was the foundation of the most important of all his works, the *Philosophical Dictionary*, which he is said to have projected in the days when he was with Frederick at Berlin. In this work he showed how a dictionary could be made the most amusing reading in the world. Under an alphabetical arrangement, he brought together a vast variety of sparkling essays on all sorts of subjects connected with literature, science, politics and religion. Some of his headings were mere stalking-horses, under cover of which he shot at the enemy. Some are concerned with matters now out of date; but, on the whole, the work presents a vivid picture of his versatile genius. An abridged edition, containing articles of abiding interest, would be a service to Free-thought at the present day.

Here is a slight specimen of his style taken from the article on Fanaticism: "Some one spreads a rumor in the world that there is a giant in existence 70 feet high. Very soon all the doctors discuss the questions what color his hair must be, what is the size of his thumb, what the dimensions of his nails; there is outcry, caballing, fighting; those who maintain that the giant's little finger is only an inch and a half in diameter, bring those to the stake who affirm that the little finger is a foot thick. 'But, gentlemen, does your giant exist?' says a bystander, modestly.

"'What a horrible doubt!' cry all the disputants; 'what blasphemy! what absurdity!' Then they all make a little truce to stone the bystander, and, after having assassinated him in due form, in a manner the most edifying, they fight among themselves, as before, on the subject of the little finger and the nails."

"L'Infâme."

Voltaire had other provocations to his attack on the bigots, and as he greatly concerned himself with these, they must be briefly mentioned. In 1761 a tragedy of mingled judicial bigotry, ignorance, and cruelty was enacted in Languedoc. On October 13th of that year, Marc Antoine, the son of Jean Calas, a respectable Protestant merchant in Toulouse, a young man of dissolute habits, who had lived the life of a scapegrace, hanged himself in his father's shop while the family were upstairs. The priestly party got hold of the case and turned it into a religious crime. The Huguenot parents were charged with murdering their son to prevent his turning Catholic. Solemn services were held for the repose of the soul of Marc Antoine, and his body was borne to the grave with more than royal pomp, as that of a martyr to the holy cause of religion. In the church of the White Penitents a hired skeleton was exhibited, holding in one hand a branch of palm, emblem of martyrdom, and in the other an inscription, in large letters, "abjuration of heresy." The populace, who were accustomed yearly to celebrate with rejoicing the Massacre of St. Bartholomew's Day, 1572, were excited against the family. The father, who for sixty years had lived without reproach, was arrested, with his wife and children. The court before whom the case was brought, at first was disposed to put the whole family to the torture, never doubting that the murder would be confessed by one or other of them. But they ended by only condemning the father to be tortured, in order to extract a confession of guilt before being broken on the wheel, after which his body was to be burned and the ashes scattered to the winds. He was submitted first to the *question ordinaire*. In sight of the rack he was asked to reveal his crime. His answer was that no crime had been committed. He was stretched on the rack until every limb was dislocated and the body drawn out several inches beyond. He was then subjected to the *question extraordinaire*. This consisted in pouring water into his mouth from a horn, while his nose was pinched, till his body was swollen to twice its size, and the sufferer endured the anguish of a hundred drownings. He submitted without flinching to all the excruciating agony. Finally, he was placed upon a tumbril and carried through the howling mob to the place of execution. "I am innocent." he muttered from time to time. At the scaffold he was exhorted to confess by a priest: "What!" said he, "you, too, believe a father can kill his own son!" They bound him to a wooden cross, and the executioner, with an iron bar, broke each of his limbs in two places, striking eleven blows in all, and then left him for two hours to die.

The executioner mercifully strangled him at last, before burning the body at the stake. To the last he persisted in his innocence: he had no confession to make. By his unutterable agony he saved the lives of his wife and family. Two daughters were thrown into a convent, and the property was confiscated. The widow and son escaped, and were provided for by Voltaire.

He spared no time, trouble, or money to arrive at the truth, and that once reached, he was as assiduous in his search for justice. He went to work with an energy and thoroughness all his own. He interested the Pompadour herself in the case. By his own efforts he forced justice to be heard. "The worst of the worthy sort of people," he said, "is that they are such cowards. A man groans over his wrong, shuts his lips, takes his supper, and forgets." Voltaire was not of that fibre. Wrong went as a knife to his heart. He suffered with the victim, and might have justly used the words of Shelley, who compared himself unto "a nerve, o'er which do creep the else unfelt oppressions of the world." Voltaire had to fire others with his own fervor. He issued pamphlet after pamphlet in which the shameful story was told with pathetic simplicity. He employed the best lawyers he could find to vindicate the memory of the murdered man. For three years he left no stone unturned, until all that was possible was done to right the foul wrong of those in authority. During this time no smile escaped him of which he did not reproach himself as a crime. Carlyle speaks of this as "Voltaire's noblest outburst, into mere transcendant blaze of pity, virtuous wrath, and determination to bring rescue and help against the whole world."

He had his pamphlets on the Calas case, seven in number, translated and published in England and Germany, where they produced a profound effect. A subscription for the Calas family was headed by the young Queen of George III. When at length judgment was given, reversing the sentence, he wrote to Damilaville: "My dear brother, there is, then, justice upon the earth! There is, then, such a thing as humanity! Men are not all wicked rascals, as they say! It is the day of your triumph, my dear brother; you have served the family better than anyone."

It was while the Calas case was pending that Voltaire composed his noble *Treatise on Toleration*, a work which, besides its great effect in Europe, caused Catherine II. to promise, if not to grant, universal religious toleration throughout the vast empire she governed.

This Calas case was scarce ended when another, almost as bad an exhibition of intolerance, occurred. Sirven, a respectable Protestant land surveyor, had a Catholic housekeeper, who, with the assent of the Bishop of Castres, spirited away his daughter for the good of her soul, and placed her in a convent, with a view to her conversion. She returned to her parents in a state of insanity, her body covered with the marks of the whip. She never recovered from the cruelties she had endured at the convent. One day, when her father was absent on his professional duties, she threw herself into a well, at the bottom of which she was found drowned. It was obvious to the authorities that the parents had murdered their child because she wished to become a Roman Catholic. They most wisely did not appear, and were sentenced to be hanged when they could be caught. In their flight the married daughter gave premature birth to a child, and Madame Sirven died in despair.

It took Voltaire eight years to get this abominable sentence reversed, and to turn wrong into right. He was now between seventy and eighty years of age, yet he threw himself into the cause of the Sirvens with the zeal and energy which has vindicated Calas; appealing to Paris and Europe, issuing pamphlets, feeing lawyers, and raising a handsome subscription for the family.

Another case was that of the Chevalier de la Barre. In 1766 a crucifix was injured—perhaps wantonly, perhaps by accident. The Bishop of Amiens called for vengeance. Two young officers were accused; one escaped, and obtained by Voltaire's request a commission in the Prussian service. The other, La Barre, was tortured to confess, and then condemned to have his tongue cut out, his hand cut off, and to be burned alive. Voltaire, seventy years old, devoted himself with untiring energy to save him. Failing in that, he wrote one of his little pamphlets, a simple, graphic *Narrative of the Death of Chevalier de la Barre*, which stirred every humane heart in France. For twelve years this infidel vindicated the memory of the murdered man and exposed his oppressors. One of the authorities concerned in this judicial atrocity threatened Voltaire with vengeance for holding them up to the execration of Europe. Voltaire replied by a Chinese anecdote. "I forbid you," said a tyrannical emperor to the historiographer, "to speak a word more of me." The mandarin began to write. "What are you doing now?" asked the emperor. "I am writing down the order that your majesty has just given me." Voltaire had sought to save Admiral Byng. He contended in a similar case at home. Count Lally had failed to save India from the English, had been taken prisoner, but allowed to go to Paris to clear his name from charges made against him. The French people, infuriate at the loss of their possession, demanded a victim, and Lally, after a process tainted with every kind of illegality, was condemned to death on the vague charge of abuse of authority. The murdered man's son, known in the Revolution as Lally Tollendal, was joined by Voltaire in the honorable work of procuring revision of the proceedings, and one of the last crowning triumphs of Voltaire's days was the news brought to him on his dying bed that his long effort had availed.

"Ecrasez L'infâme."

These are samples of what was occuring when Voltaire was exhorting his friends to *crush the infamous*—a phrase which gave rise to much misunderstanding, and which priests have even alleged was applied to Jesus, their idol. A sufficient disproof, if any were needed, is that Voltaire treats "l'infâme" as feminine. *Si vous pouvez écraser l'infâme, ecrasez-la, et aimez-moi." That oft-repeated phrase was directed at no person. Nor was it, as some Protestants have alleged, directed only at Roman Catholicism. As Voltaire saw and said, "fanatic Papists and fanatic Calvanism are tarred with one brush." "L'infâme" was Christian superstition claiming supernatural authority and enforcing its claim, as it has ever sought to do, by pains and penalties. He meant by it the whole spirit of exclusiveness, intolerance, and bigotry, persecuting and privileged orthodoxy, which he saw-as the outcome of the divine faith. Practically, as D. F. Strauss justly remarked, "when Voltaire writes to D'Alembert that he wishes to see the 'Infâme' reduced in France to the same condition in which she finds herself in England, and when Frederick writes to Voltaire that philosophers flourished amongst the Greeks and Romans, because their religion had no dogmas— '*mais les dogmes de notre infâme gâtent tout'*—it is clear we must understand by the 'Infâme,' whose destruction was the watchword of the Voltairian circle, the Christian Church, without distinction of communions, Catholic or Protestant."

The Catholic Joseph de Maistre shrieks: "With a fury without example, this insolent blasphemer declared himself the personal enemy of the Savior of men, dared from the depths of his nothingness to give him a name of ridicule, and that adorable law which the Man-God brought to earth he called 'l'infame.'" This is a judgment worthy of a bigot, who dares not look into the reason why his creed is detested. Let us try and understand this insolent blasphemer to-day.

Voltaire looked deep into the heart of the atrocities that wrung his every nerve with anguish. They were not new: only the humanity and courage that assailed them were new. They were the natural outcome of what had been Christian teaching. It was not simply that, as a matter of fact, priests and theologians were the opponents of every kind of rational progress, but their intolerance was the logical result of their creed. These atrocities could not have been perpetrated had not priests and magistrates had behind them a credulous and fanatical populace, whose minds were suborned from childhood to believing that they had themselves the one and divine faith, and that all heretics were enemies of God. He saw that to destroy the intolerance he must sap the superstition from which it sprang. He saw that the core of the Christian superstition lay in Bibliolatry, and that while Christians believed they had an exclusive and infallibly divine revelation, they would deem all opposition to their own beliefs a sin, meriting punishment. Mr. Morley says, with truth: "If we find ourselves walking amid a generation of cruel, unjust, and darkened spirits, we may be assured that it is their beliefs on what they deem highest that have made them so. There is no counting with certainty on the justice of men who are capable of fashioning and worshipping an unjust divinity; nor on their humanity, so long as they incorporate inhuman motives in their most sacred dogma; nor on their reasonableness, while they rigorously decline to accept reason as a test of truth."

Voltaire warred on Christian superstition because he keenly felt its evils. He saw that intolerance naturally flowed from the exclusive and dogmatic claims which alone differentiated it from other faiths. Its inducements to right-doing he found to be essentially ignoble, appealing either to brutal fear of punishment or base expectation of reward, and in each case alike mercenary. He saw that terrorism engendered brutality, that a savage will think nothing of slaughtering hundreds to appease his angry God. He saw that it had been a fine religion for priests and monks—those caterpillars of the commonwealth, living on the fat of the land while pretending to hold the keys of heaven, a race of parasites on the people, who toil not neither do they spin, and whose direct interest lay in fostering their dupes ignorance and credulity. The Christian tree was judged, as its founder said it should be, by its fruits. Men do not gather grapes from thorns, or figs from thistles. He saw Christianity as Tacitus described it—"a maleficent superstition." It was a upas tree, to be cut down; and hence he reiterated his terrible *Delenda est Carthago*, "Ecrasez l'Infâme"—"Destroy the monster."

He wrote to D'Alembert from Ferney: "For forty years I have endured the outrages of bigots and scoundrels. I have found there is nothing to gain by moderation, and that it is a deception. I must wage war openly and die nobly, 'on a crowd of bigots slaughtered at my feet.'" His war was relentless and unremitting. He assailed "l'Infâme" with every weapon which learning, wit, industry, and indignation could supply.

Frederick wrote to him from the midst of his own wars: "Your zeal burns against the Jesuits and superstitions. You do well to combat error, but do you credit that the world will change? The human mind is weak. Three-fourths of mankind are formed to be the slaves of the absurdest fanaticism. The fear of the devil and hell is fascinating to them, and they detest the sage who wishes to enlighten them. I look in vain among them for the image of God, of which the theologians assure us they carry the imprint." Madame du Deffand wrote in a similar strain. She assured him that every person of sense thought as he did; why then continue? No remonstrance moved him. He had enlisted for the war, and might have said with Luther: *Hier stehe ich; ich kann nicht anders.*

Much nonsense has been written about Voltaire's employment of ridicule against religious beliefs. I am reminded of Bishop South's remark to a dull brother bishop, who reproved him for sprinkling his sermon with witticisms.

"Now, my lord, do you really mean to say that, if God had given you any wit, you would not have used it?" Voltaire ridiculed what he esteemed ridiculous. But there is nothing more galling to superstitionists than to find that others find food for mirth in their absurdities.

"You mock at sacred things," said the Jesuits to Pascal when he exposed their casuistry. Doubtless the priests of Baal said the same when Elijah asked them whether their God was asleep, or peradventure on a journey. The artifice of inculcating a solemn and reverential manner of treating absurdities is the perennial recipe for sanctifying and perpetuating superstition. "Priests of all persuasions," says Oliver Goldsmith, "are enemies to ridicule, because they know it to be a formidable antagonist to fanaticism, and they preach up gravity to conceal their own shallowness of imposture." Approach the mysteries of the faith with reverence and you concede half the battle. Christian missionaries do not thus treat the fetishism and sorcery of heathen lands. To overcome it they must expose its absurdities. Ridicule has been a weapon in the hands of all the great liberators, Luther, Erasmus, Rabelais, Bruno, Swift, but none used it more effectively than Voltaire. Buckle well says; "He used ridicule, not as the test of truth, but as the scourge of folly." And he adds: "His irony, his wit, his pungent and telling sarcasms produce more effect than the gravest arguments could have done; and there can be no doubt he was fully justified in using those great resources with which nature had endowed him, since by their aid he advanced the interests of truth, and relieved men from some of their most inveterate prejudices." Victor Hugo puts the case in poetic fashion when he declares that Voltaire was irony incarnate for the salvation of mankind. "Ridicule is not argument"! Well, it is a pointed form of polemic, the *argumentum ad absurdum*. "Mustapha," said Voltaire, "does not believe, but he believes that he believes." To shame him out of hypocrisy, there is nothing better than laughter; and if a true believer, laughter will best free him from terror of his bogey devil and no less bogey god. Ridicule can hurt no reality. You cannot make fun of the multiplication table. The fun begins when the theologians assert that three times one are one. Shaftesbury, who maintained that ridicule was a test of truth, remarked with justice, "'tis the persecuting spirit that has raised the bantering one." Ridicule is the natural retort to those who seek not to convert but to convict and punish. Ridicule comes like a stream of sunlight to dissipate the fogs of preconceived prejudice. A laugh, if no argument, is a splendid preparative. Often, in Voltaire, ridicule takes an argumentative form. Thus, alluding to a Monsieur Esprit's book on the Falsity of Human Virtues, he says: "That great genius, Mons. Esprit, tells us that neither Cato, Aristotle, Marcus Aurelius, nor Epictetus were good men, and a good reason why, good men are only found among Christians. Again, among the Christians, Catholics alone are virtuous, and of the Catholics, the Jesuits, enemies of the Oratorians, must be excepted. Therefore, there is scarce any virtue on earth, except among the enemies of the Jesuits."

All his characteristic scorn and ridicule come out when dealing with the fetish book of his adversaries. The *Philosophical Dictionary* is full of wit upon biblical subjects. I content myself with an excerpt from the less known *Sermon of Fifty*: "If Moses changed the waters into blood, the sages of Pharoah did the same. He made frogs come upon the land; this also they were able to do. But when lice were concerned, they were vanquished; in the matter of lice, the Jews knew more and could do more than the other nations."

"Finally, Adonaï caused every first-born in Egypt to die, in order that his people might be at their ease. For his people the sea is cloven in twain; and we must confess it is the least that could be done on this occasion. All the other marvels are of the same stamp. The Jews wander in the desert. Some husbands complain of their wives. Immediately water is found, which makes every woman who has been faithless to her husband swell and burst. In the desert the Jews have neither bread nor dough, but quails and manna are rained upon them. Their clothes are preserved unworn for forty years; as the children grow, their clothes grow with them. Samson, because he had not undergone the operation of shaving, defeats a thousand Philistines with the jaw-bone of an ass. He ties together three hundred foxes, which, as a matter of course, come quite readily to his hand.

"There is scarcely a page in which tales of this sort are not found. The ghost of Samuel appears, summoned by the voice of a witch. The shadow of a dial—as if miserable creatures like the Jews had dials—goes back ten degrees at the prayer of Hezekiah, who, with great judgment, asks for this sign. God gives him the choice of making the hour advance or recede, and the learned Hezekiah thinks that it is not difficult to make the shadow advance, but very difficult to make it recede. Elijah mounts to heaven in a chariot of fire; children sing in a hot and raging furnace. I should never stop if I entered into the detail of all the monstrous extravagances with which this book swarms. Never was common sense outraged so vehemently and indecently." Noticing the comparison in the Song of Solomon, "Her nose is like the tower of Damascus," etc., he says: "This, I own, is not in the style of the Eclogues of the author of the Æneid; but all have not a like style, and a Jew is not obliged to write like Virgil."

This, it may be objected, is caricature and not criticism. But all that Voltaire sought was that his blows should tell. He did not expect to be taken *au pied du lettre*. Some of his biblical criticism is faulty, but it is hard for the reader to recover from the tone of banter and contempt with which he treats the sacred book. When the idol is shattered, it is not much use saying its mouth was not quite so big and ugly as it was represented to be. Priests have never yet been troubled by dull criticism. They left Tindal and Chubb alone; but when Woolston, Annet and Paine added liveliness to their infidelity, they loudly called for the police.

Leslie Stephen well says: "Men have venerated this or that grotesque monstrosity because they have always approached it with half-shut eyes and grovelling on their faces in the dust: a single hearty laugh will encourage them to stand erect and to learn the latest of lessons—that of seeing what lies before them. And if your holy religion does really depend upon preserving the credit of Jonah's whale, upon justifying all the atrocities of the Jews, and believing that a census was punished by a plague, ridicule is not only an effective but an appropriate mode of argument."

Voltaire is often sneered at as a mere destructive. The charge is not true, and, even if it were, he would none the less deserve the admiration of posterity for his destructive work. It is as necessary for the gardener to clear away the rubbish and keep down the weeds as to sow and water. Mr. Morley justly observes: "He had imagination enough and intelligence enough to perceive that they are the most pestilent of all the enemies of mankind, the sombre hierarchs of misology, who take away the keys of knowledge, thrusting truth down to the second place, and discrowning sovereign reason to be the serving drudge of superstition or social usuage."

Voltaire was the arch iconoclast of his age, a mere destructive, if you will. Buckie truly remarks: "All great reforms have consisted, not in making something new, but in unmaking something old." W. J. Fox eloquently said: "The destruction of tyranny is political freedom. The destruction of bigotry is spiritual and mental emancipation. Positive and negative are mere forms. Creation and destruction, as we call them, are just one and the same work, the work which man has to do—the extraction of good from evil."

Much has been made of the pseudonymous character of his attacks on Christianity, and of the subterfuges and fibs with which he sought to evade responsibility. One might as well complain of ironclads wearing armor in warfare.

It was the necessity of his position. He wanted to do his work, not to become a martyr, leaving it to unknown hands. It should be remembered that Voltaire had sometimes to bribe publishers to bring out his writings; and, in such circumstances, the pseudonymity is surely open to no suspicion of baseness. His poem on *Natural Religion* was condemned to the flames by the decree of the Parliament of Paris, 23rd January, 1759. His *Important Examination of the Scriptures*, which he falsely attributed to Lord Bolingbroke, was condemned with five other of his pieces by a decree of the Court of Rome, 29th November, 1771. Could the author have been caught, he would have had a good chance, if not of sharing the fate of his book, at least of permanent lodgment in the Bastille, of which he had already sufficient taste. He knew that although Bolingbroke had no hand in its composition he largely shared its ideas, and he obtained at once publicity and security by attributing it to the dead friend who, Morley says, "was the direct progenitor of Voltaire's opinions in religion." If he stuck at no subterfuge to achieve his work, his lies injured no one. One of the funniest was the signing one of his heterodox publications as the Archbishop of Canterbury, a lie which may remind us of the drunken Sheridan announcing himself as William Wilberforce. Voltaire had been Bastilled twice, and verily believed that another taste would end his days. "I am," he said, "a friend of truth, but no friend at all to martyrdom." Shelter behind any ambush was necessary in such guerilla warfare as his. Over fifty of his works were condemned, and placed upon the Index. Voltaire used no fewer than one hundred and thirty different pen-names, which have enabled bibliographers to display their erudition.(1) But for this underground method, he might have been laid by the heels instead of living to old age, with the satisfaction of seeing the world becoming a little more humane and tolerant through his efforts. In such warfare the only test is success, and the fact remains that Voltaire's blows told. He cleared the course for modern science, and it is not for those who benefit by his labors to sneer because he did not become a martyr in the struggle.

1. Special mention should be made of the *Bibliographie Voltairienne* of M. L. Querard, and *Voltaire: Bibliographie de ses Œuvres*, in four volumes, by M. G. Bengesco, 1882- 1890.

Condorcet says: "His zeal against a religion which he regarded as the cause of the fanaticism which has desolated Europe since its birth, of the superstition which had burst about it, and as the source of the mischief which the enemies of human nature still continued to do, seemed to double his activity and his forces. 'I am tired,' he said one day, 'of hearing it repeated that twelve men were enough to establish Christianity. I want to show them that one will be enough to destroy it.'" What one man could do he did. But it took not twelve legendary apostles, but the labor of countless thousands of men, through many ages, to build up the great complex of Christianity, and it will need the labors of as many to destroy it. Voltaire himself came to see this, and wrote, in the year before his death, "I now perceive that we must still wait three or four hundred years. One day it cannot but be that good men will win their cause; but before that glorious day arrives, how many disgusts have we to undergo, how many dark persecutions, without reckoning the La Barres of whom they will make an *auto de fe* from time to time."

John Morley remarks: "The meaner partisans of an orthodoxy, which can only make wholly sure of itself by injustice to adversaries, has always loved to paint the Voltairean school in the characters of demons, enjoying their work of destruction with a sportive and impish delight. They may have rejoiced in their strength so long as they cherished the illusion that those who first kindled the torch should also complete the long course and bear the lamp to the goal. When the gravity of the enterprise showed itself before them, they remained alert with all courage, but they ceased to fancy that courage necessarily makes men happy. The mantle of philosophy was rent in a hundred places, and bitter winds entered at a hundred holes; but they only drew it the more closely around them."

It may remain an inspiration to others, as it assuredly is a proof of the temperance and moderation of his own life, that much of Voltaire's best work was done after he had reached his sixtieth year. *Candide*, his masterpiece, was written at the age of sixty-four. Four years later he produced his *Sermon of the Fifty*, and he was sixty-nine when he published his epoch-making *Treatise upon Toleration*, and *Saul*, the wittiest of his burlesque dramas. At the age of seventy he issued his most important work, the *Philosophical Dictionary*, and his burlesque upon existing superstitions, which he entitled *Pot-Pourri*. This was, indeed, the period of his greatest literary activity against "l'Infame." His *Questions on the Miracles*, his *Examination of Lord Bolingbroke*, the *Questions of Zapata*, the *Dinner of Count de Boulainvilliers* (the charming *resumé* of Voltaire's religious opinions, which had the honor to be burnt by the hand of the hangman), the *Canonisation of St. Cucufin*, the romance of the *Princess of Babylon*, the *A. B. and C.*, the collection of *Ancient Gospels*, and his *God and Men*, all being issued while he was between seventy and seventy-five. It was at this time he edited the *Recueil Nécessaire avec l'Evangile de la Raison*, a collection of anti-Christian tracts dated Leipsic and London, but printed at Amsterdam. He was eighty when he put forth his *White Bull* (one of the funniest of his pieces, which was translated by Jeremy Bentham), and his ridiculous skit on Bababec and the Fakirs; eighty-two when he wrote *The Bible Explained* and *A Christian against Six Jews*; and eighty-three when he published his *History of the Establishment of Christianity*.

It was thus in the last twenty years of his long life that Voltaire did his best work for the destruction of prejudice and the spread of enlightenment. At the same time he maintained a large correspondence, both with the principal sovereigns of Europe, whom he urged in the direction of tolerance, and with the leading writers, whom he wished to combine in a great and systematic attempt to sap the creed he believed to be at the root of superstition and intolerance.

It is in his lengthy and varied correspondence with intimates, extending over sixty years, that Voltaire most truly reveals himself. He is therein his own minute biographer, revealing not only his actions, but their actuation. We see him therein not merely the prince of *persifleurs*, but the serious sensitive thinker, keenly alive to friendship, love, and work for the higher interests of humanity. His letters are among the most varied, interesting, and delightful of any left by a great man of letters. Like all his other productions, they display the fertility of his genius. Over ten thousand separate letters are catalogued by Bengesco. Their very extent prevents their being widely read, but they reveal the perennial brightness of his mind, his delight in work, his love of literature and liberty, his constant gaiety and goodness of heart, with here and there only a flash of indignation and contempt. They are imbued with the spirit of friendship, abound in anecdotes and pleasantries, mingled with a passionate earnestness for the interest of mankind. Constantly we find him endeavoring to elevate the literary class, to raise the drama, continually seeking to encourage talent, to relieve suffering, and to defend the oppressed.

LAST DAYS

WITH the authorities at Geneva Voltaire had got into dispute, owing to his attempt to establish a private theatre in the territory still dominated by the ghost of Calvin. Moreover, he was continually reminding them of Servetus. When D'Alembert's article on Geneva appeared the citizens were enraged, and Voltaire thought proper to also purchase an estate near Lausanne, in the Vaud Canton, which was somewhat less austere in theatrical matters. Here Gibbon was also residing at the time.

Stupid stories have been told of Gibbon's attempts to see Voltaire, and of their mutual laughter at each other's ugliness. Voltaire is said to have refused himself to the young Englishman, which is very unlikely, and that he replied: "You are like the Christian God: he permits one to eat and drink, but will never show himself." It is said that he got Voltaire's mare let loose on purpose to see the old man chase after him. Voltaire sent a servant to charge him twelve sous for seeing the great beast, whereupon he gave twenty-four, with the remark, "that will pay for a second visit." Gibbon himself, speaking of the winter of 1757-58, which he spent in the neighborhood of Lausanne, says: "My desire of beholding Voltaire, whom I then rated above his real magnitude, was easily gratified. He received me with civility as an English youth, but I cannot boast of any peculiar notice or distinction. The highest gratification which I derived from Voltaire's residence at Lausanne was the uncommon circumstance of hearing a great poet declaim his own productions on the stage. He had formed a company of gentlemen and ladies, some of whom were not destitute of talents. My ardor, which soon became conspicuous, seldom failed of procuring me a ticket.... The wit and philosophy of Voltaire, his table and theatre, refined in a visible degree the manners of Lausanne; and, however addicted to study, I enjoyed my share of the amusements of society."

This taste for directing theatrical representations was shared, perhaps we might say followed, by his great German admirer Goethe. It was Voltaire's relaxation. One of his most particular friends was the great actor Le Kain. The drama was with him an instrument of education. He believed it to be a means both of softening and refining manners, and also of dispersing intolerance and superstition.

Voltaire soon afterwards purchased a third estate at Ferney, just a little over the French border, and here, eventually, he lived *en grande seigneur*, and was known as the "patriarch of Ferney." A philosopher, he said, with hounds at his heels, like a fox should never trust to one hole. Accordingly, he had within easy distance the choice of three distinct governments wherein to find a place of refuge, for, as Carlyle remarks, he "had to keep his eyes open and always have covert within reach, under pain of being torn to pieces, while he went about in the flesh, or rather in the bones, poor lean being." He now had wealth, independence, and an assurance of safety, and had come to that time of life when most men who are able think they may fairly retire from their labors. But now was the time when he, casting aside all other pleasures and ambitions, threw himself with unflagging energy and unsurpassed industry into the great task of his life. It was from Ferney he issued all the remarkable works of his later years.

At Ferney, the old church obstructing his view of the Alps, he built a new one, and got into trouble for doing so. He had inscribed on it, "Deo erexit Voltaire, 1761," a phrase which betrayed rather patronage than devotion.

"It is," he remarked, "the only church dedicated to God alone; all the others are dedicated to saints. For my part, I would rather worship the master than the valets." On another occasion, he said: "Yes, I adore God; but not monsieur his son, and madame his mother." It was observed of the inscription that he had only a single word between himself and God. From the wall of his church he also built a tomb for himself. "The wicked will say that I am neither inside nor outside," he remarked. Of the church he remarked: "The wicked will say, no doubt, that I am building this church in order to throw down the one which conceals a beautiful prospect, and to have a grand avenue; but I let the impious talk, and go on working out my salvation." If the wicked made the remarks predicted, they doubtless spoke the truth. It was even reported that Voltaire personally superintended the removal of the old ruinous one, saying, "Take away that gibbet" when pointing to the crucifix. The *cure* of Moens, the parish adjoining Ferney, cited Voltaire before the ecclesiastical official of Gex as guilty of impiety and sacrilege, and Wagnière, Voltaire's secretary, says: "Those gentlemen indulged the confident hope that M. de Voltaire would be burned, or at least hanged, for the greater glory of God and the edification of the faithful. This they said publicly." Voltaire was enabled to strike terror to his persecutor by producing a royal ordinance of 1627 forbidding a *cure* to serve either as prosecutor or judge in such cases. The church remains, but the celebrated inscription was effaced during the Restoration of the Monarchy.

Ferney became an asylum for the oppressed both from France and Switzerland. Many of these Voltaire located in and about his château, but, as their number increased, he built nice stone houses, and, in a little time, the miserable hamlet which before his arrival had been a wilderness, became a prosperous colony of twelve hundred individuals and a veritable free State. There were both Protestants and Catholics among them, but such was the unanimity in which they lived under his protection, that we are told no one could conceive that different religions existed among them. Among this colony he established the manufacture of weaving and of watches, by means of which his people presently became wealthy; the Empress Catherine II., even when engaged in her Turkish campaigns, paying her *bon ami* Voltaire the compliment of assisting the Ferney colony by an order for watches to the value of some thousand roubles. He pushed the work of his colonists into repute throughout the world, and was justified in saying to the Duke of Richelieu, "Give me a fair chance, and I am the man to build a city."

Though everywhere maligned as an infidel and a scoffer, his life was one long act of benevolence. The watches of Ferney became known as those of Geneva. "Fifteen years ago," said a visitor, "there were barely at Ferney three or four cottages and forty inhabitants; now it is astonishing to see a numerous and civilised colony, a theatre, and more than a hundred pretty houses." "His charities," says General Hamley, "were munificent. When the Order of Jesuits was suppressed he took one of the body, Father Adam, into his house, and made him his almoner, a post which was far from being a sinecure." Hearing that Mademoiselle Corneille, the grandniece of the poet, was in poverty, Voltaire, in the most delicate manner, invited her to his house, treated her as a relation, and gave her an education suitable to her descent. "It is," he said, "the duty of an old soldier to be useful to the daughter of his general." That she might not feel under personal obligation, he devoted to her dowry the profits of his *Commentaries on Corneille*.

"A description is given of him in his last days at Ferney, seated under a vine, on the occasion of a *fête*, and receiving the congratulations and complimentary gifts of his tenantry and neighbors, when a young lady, whom he had adopted, brought him in a basket a pair of white doves with pink beaks, as her offering. He afterwards entertained about 200 guests at a splendid repast, followed by illuminations, songs, and dances, and was himself so carried away in an access of gaiety as to throw his hat into the air. But his merriment ended in a tempest of wrath; for learning, in the course of the evening, that the two doves which had figured so prettily in the *fête* had been killed for the table, his indignation at the stolid cruelty which could shed the blood of the creatures they had all just admired and caressed, knew no bounds."

Diderot, who shares with Voltaire the glory of being the intellectual landmark of last century, and who equalled him as an artist and excelled him as a philosopher, only met Voltaire a little before his death. The fame of Voltaire's wealth had kept him from Ferney. Speaking of Voltaire in old age, Diderot says: "He is like one of those old haunted castles, which are falling into ruins in every part; but you easily perceive that it is inhabited by some ancient magician." Diderot was the better critic, and controverted the patriarch as to the merits of Shakespeare, whom he compared to the statue of Saint Christopher at Notre Dame—unshapely and rude; but: such a colossus that ordinary petty men could pass between his legs without touching him.

Late in life, Voltaire adopted Reine Philiberte de Vericourt, a young girl of noble but poor family, whom he had rescued from a convent life, installed in his own house, and married to the Marquis de Villette. Her pet name was *Belle et Bonne*, and no one had more to do with the happiness of the last years of Voltaire than she. She watched by the dying Voltaire's bedside, and Lady Morgan thus records her report: "To his last moment everything he said and did breathed the benevolence and goodness of his character. All announced in him tranquility, peace, resignation; except a little moment of ill-humor which he showed to the *cure* of St. Sulpice when he begged him to withdraw, and said, 'Let me die in peace.'"

Voltaire himself wrote to Mme. du Deffand: "They say sometimes of a man, 'He died like a dog'; but, truly, a dog is very happy to die without all the ceremony with which they persecute the last moments of our lives. If they had a little charity for us, they would let us die without saying anything about it. The worst is that we are then surrounded by hypocrites, who worry us to make us think as they do not in the least think; or else by imbeciles, who desire us to be as stupid as they are. All this is very disgusting. The only pleasure of life at Geneva is that people can die there as they like; many worthy persons summon no priest at all. People kill themselves if they please, without any one objecting; or they await the last moment, and no one troubles them about it."

Under suffering, age, and impending death, Voltaire's bearing, as Carlyle acknowledges, "one must say is rather beautiful." Voltaire had all his life "enjoyed" bad health. He had always a feeble constitution, and was a confirmed invalid for the greater part of his life, suffering from bladder disorder, and a variety of other diseases that would have soon finished an ordinary man. We may say he was sustained by his work, which was ever gay, even when most pessimistic. "My eyes are as red as a drunkard's," he writes, "and I have not the honor to be one." His wit lasted in old age. A visitor to Ferney, hearing him praise Haller enthusiastically, told him that Haller did not do him equal justice. "Ah," said Voltaire, lightly, "perhaps we are both mistaken." To Bailly, the astronomer, he wrote, at the age of eighty-one: "A hundred thanks for the book of medicine which you sent me, together with your own [*History of Ancient Astronomy*], when I was very unwell. I have not opened the first. The second I have read and feel much better." He kept himself at work with coffee. His interest was ever in his work. At the very last, the new dictionary he had proposed to the Academy was on his mind; it was not proceeding as rapidly as his indefatigable spirit desired. "J'ai fait un pen de bien; c'est mon meilleur ouvrage"—"I have done a little good; that is my best work," was one of his latest utterances.

His physicians gave their opinion that he might have lived even longer than he did had he not been lured to Paris by his niece (unprepossessing Madame

Denis) to superintend the production of his last tragedy *Irene*. Asked at the barrier if there was anything contraband in the carriage, he replied, "Only myself." On entering Paris he received a shock in the news that his friend Le Kain, the actor, had been buried the day before. He was visited by Benjamin Franklin, who brought his grandson, whom they desired to kneel for the patriarch's blessing. Pronouncing in English the words, "God, Liberty, Toleration"—"this," said Voltaire, "is the most suitable benediction for the grandson of Franklin." Poems, addresses and deputations came thick upon him, and his hotel was thronged with visitors of rank and eminence. The popular voice hailed the aged patriarch, especially as the defender of Calas, the apostle of universal toleration; and this title was more gratifying to him than any other.

In one house where Voltaire called on his last visit to Paris, the mistress reproached him for the obstinacy with which, in extreme old age (over eighty-three), he continued to assail the Church and its beliefs. "Be moderate and generous," said she, "after the victory. What can you fear now from such adversaries? The fanatics are prostrate (*à terre*). They can no longer injure. Their reign is over." Voltaire replied: "You are in error, madame; it is a fire that is covered but not extinguished. Those fanatics, those Tartuffes, are mad dogs. They are muzzled, but they have not lost their teeth. It is true they bite no more; but on the first opportunity, if their teeth are not drawn, you will see if they will not bite." All that one man could do was done by Voltaire. More than any other, he helped to muzzle the mad dog of religious intolerance, lassoing it dexterously with his finespun silken thread, since replaced by a stronger cord. But the beast even yet is not dead; its teeth are not all drawn. Give it a chance and it will still bite. What we have to thank Voltaire for is, that he has left works which, as he himself said, are "scissors and files to file the teeth and pare the talons of the monsters."

Voltaire was, as he said, stifled in roses. He sat up at night perfecting *Irene*, and his unwearied activity induced him at his great age to begin a Dictionary upon a novel plan which he prevailed upon the French Academy to take up. At the performance of his tragedy he was crowned with laurel in his box, amid the plaudits of the audience. To keep himself up under the excitement, he exceeded even his usual excess of coffee. These labors and dissipation brought on spitting of blood, and sleeplessness, to obviate which he took opium. Condorcet says the servant mistook one of the doses, which threw him into a state of lethargy, from which he never recovered. He lingered for some time, but at length expired on the 30th of May, 1778, in his eighty-fourth year.

Of course lying tales of dying horrors were floated, and disbelieved in by all who knew him. He wished to rest in his own churchyard, and let the *abbé* Gaultier and the *curé* de St. Sulpice squabble as to who should have, the honor of his conversion. His secretary, being alone with him, begged him to state what his view continued to be when he believed himself dying; and received this written declaration: "I die adoring God, loving my friends, not hating my enemies, detesting superstition"—"Je meurs eti adorant dieu, en aimant mes amis, en ne baissant pas mes ennemis, de testant superstition." This dying declaration may be seen at the *Bibliothèque Nationale*, Paris (Fr. 11,460), written, signed and dated by him in a still firm hand, February, 1778.

Into the stories told of Voltaire's dying moments and many similar legends, my colleague, Mr. G. W. Foote, has fully entered in his *Infidel Deathbeds*. He quotes the following extract from a letter by Dr. Burard, who, as assistant physician, was constantly about Voltaire in his last moments:

"I feel happy in being able, while paying homage to truth, to destroy the effect of the lying stories which have been told respecting the last moments of Mons. de Voltaire. I was, by office, one of those who were appointed to watch the whole progress of his illness, with MM. Tron-chin, Lorry, and Try, his medical attendants. I never left him for an instant during his last moments, and I can certify that we invariably observed in him the same strength of character, though his disease was necessarily attended with horrible pain. (Here follow the details of his case.) We positively forbade him to speak, in order to prevent the increase of a spitting of blood, with which he was attacked; still he continued to communicate with us by means of little cards, on which he wrote his questions; we replied to him verbally, and if he was not satisfied, he always made his observations to us in writing. He therefore retained his faculties up to the last moment, and the fooleries which have been attributed to him are deserving of the greatest contempt. It could not even be said that such or such person had related any circnmstance of his death, as being witness to it; for at the last, admission to his chamber was forbidden to any person. Those who came to obtain intelligence respecting the patient, waited in the saloon, and other apartments at hand. The proposition, therefore, which has been put in the mouth of Marshal Richelieu is as unfounded as the rest.

"Paris, April 3rd, 1819.

"(Signed) Burard."

The actual facts are thus told by Mr. Parton: "Ten minutes before he breathed his last he roused from his slumber, took the hand of his valet, pressed it, and said to him: 'Adieu, my dear Morand; I am dying.' These were his last words."

D'Alembert, in a letter to Frederick, written after Voltaire's death, thus recorded the impression made on him by the dying man. Having described the stupefying effects of the opium which left his head clear only for brief intervals, D'Alembert, who saw him during one of them, proceeds: "He recognised me and even spoke to me some friendly words. But the moment after he fell back into his state of stupor, for he was almost always dying. He awoke only to complain and to say 'he had come to Paris to die.'" Throughout his illness, D'Alembert adds, "he exhibited, to the extent which his condition permitted, much tranquility of mind, although he seemed to regret life. I saw him again the day before his death, and to some friendly words of mine he replied, pressing my hand, 'You are my consolation.'"

It is certain the heads of the French Church did not consider that Voltaire had made a death-bed conversion, for they refused his body burial in consecrated ground. They had anathematised him when alive and proscribed him when dead. He had prepared a tomb for himself under the sky, where he had grown old and done good, but he was cheated out of his rights, and it was decided that he who built the church had no right to have his bones bleach in the cemetery. Letters were sent to the Bishop of Annecy, in whose diocese Ferney was, enjoining him to prohibit the *cure* thereof from giving Voltaire's remains Christian burial in his own churchyard. Voltaire's nephew, the *abbé* Mignot, held a ruined abbey at Scillieres, in Champagne, a hundred miles or so from Paris; and here the body was secretly hurried off and interred. On the very day of interment the Bishop of the diocese wrote to the Prior forbidding the burial. There was even some talk of having the body exhumed, and the clergy clamored for the expulsion of the Prior. Grimm relates that "the players were forbidden to act M. de Voltaire's pieces till further orders, the editors of the public papers to speak of his death in any terms, either favorable or unfavorable, and the preceptors of the colleges to suffer any of their scholars to learn his verses."

In 1791, by a decree of the National Assembly and amid the acclamation of the people, his body was brought and placed in the Pantheon, where it rested beside that of Rousseau. At the Restoration in 1814 some bigoted Royalist stole away the bones, which were thrown into a hole with lime poured on them.

In person Voltaire was always slim, with the long head which, Carlyle says, "is the best sign of intelligence." His thinness is commemorated by the poor but well-known epigram attributed to Young, and identifying him at once with "Satan, Death, and Sin." In old age he became a mere skeleton, with eyes of great brilliancy peering beneath his wig. He was sober and temperate save in coffee, which he drank as inveterately as Johnson did tea. Conversation and literature were, as with Johnson, the gods of his idolatry.

HIS CHARACTER AND SERVICES

BOLINGBROKE finely said of Marlborough: "He was so great a man that I forget his errors." One can as justly say the same of Voltaire. I have scant sympathy with those who, dealing with great men, seek every opportunity of bringing them down to the common level. Voltaire was by no means a faultless character. He was far indeed from being an immaculate hero: he had the failings of his age and of his training. But they form no essential part of his work. How much has been made of the coarseness and immorality of Luther by men like Father Anderdon! All men have the defects of their qualities. Condorcet, in his *Life of Voltaire*, has placed on record this just criticism: "The happy qualities of Voltaire were often obscured and distorted by a natural mobility, aggravated by the habit of writing tragedies. He passed in a moment from anger to sympathetic emotion; from indignation to pleasantry. His passions, naturally violent, sometimes transported him too far; and his excessive mobility deprived him of the advantages ordinarily attached to passionate tempers—firmness in conduct—courage which no terrors can withhold from action, and which no dangers, anticipated beforehand, can shake by their actual presence. Voltaire has often been seen to expose himself rashly to the storm—seldom to meet it with fortitude. These alternations of audacity and weakness have often afflicted his friends, and prepared unworthy triumphs for his envenomed enemies."

He was too ready to lash the curs who barked at his heels, thereby stimulating them to further noise. Scandalous ex-Jesuit Desfontaines, L'Ane de Mirepoix, Thersites Fréron and the rest, would be forgotten had he not condescended to apply the whip. Voltaire was always something of a spoilt child, over-sensitive to every reproach. His petulance impelled him to absurd displays of weakness and frenzy, which he was the first to regret. He was generous even to his enemies when they were in trouble. The weaknesses of Voltaire were, like his smile, on the surface, but there was a great human heart beating beneath.

The restlessness of Voltaire has been contrasted with the repose of Goethe, and Gallic fury with calm Teutonic strength. But which of the two men did most for humanity? Voltaire might have been as calm as Goethe had he been indifferent to everything but his own culture and comfort. No! he loved the fight. When the battle of freedom raged, there was he in the thick of it, considering not his reputation, but what he could do to crush the infamous. An enemy said of him: "He is the first man in the world at writing down what other people have thought." Mr. Morley justly considers this high and sufficient praise.

The life of a writer was defined by Pope as "a warfare upon earth." Never was this truer than in the case of Voltaire, who himself said: *"La vie à'un homme de lettres est un combat perpétuel et on meurt les armes à la main."* He was ever in the midst of the fight, and usually alone and surrounded by enemies. And his unfailing resources not merely kept them at bay, but compelled their surrender of an immense territory. His was a life of creation and contest. In the war against despotism and Christianity he achieved a new kingship of public opinion, and proved that the pen was indeed mightier than the sword.

Heine said: "We should forgive our enemies—but not until they are hung." Voltaire forgave his when he had gibbeted them in his writings. People who find it difficult to understand his bitterness against "L'Infâme" should remember the revolting cruelty of which religious bigotry was still capable in his day. The Revocation of the Edict of Nantes, the prolonged horrors of the Thirty Years' War, and the Massacre of St. Bartholomew vibrated still. Condorcet wrote: "The blood of many millions of men, massacred in the name of God, still steams up to heaven around us. The earth on which we tread is everywhere covered with the bones of the victims of barbarous intolerance." His rhetoric expressed the feeling of a generation who knew by experience the evils of religious bigotry and fanaticism.

It is as a champion of Freethought that Voltaire deserves chiefly to be remembered. In that capacity I can only find words of praise. Complaints of his flippancy, his *persiflage*, his ridicule, his scurrility, his etc., came, and still come, from the enemy, and show that his blows told and tell. If he did not crush the infamous he at least crippled it. No doubt, under different circumstances,

Voltaire would have fought differently. But he would never have thought of treating atrocities without indignation, or absurdities without ridicule. Gravity is a part of the game of imposture, and there is nothing the hypocrites and humbugs resent so much as having their solemn pretensions laughed at.
.

He knew the subtle power of ridicule. It was the most effective weapon, not only for the time and the nation in which he wrote, but for our time also. His blows were all dealt with grace and agility; his pills were sugar-coated. Grimm well said of him: "He makes arrows of every kind of wood, brilliant and rapid in their flight, but with a keen, unerring point. Under his sparkling pen, erudition ceases to be ponderous and becomes full of life. If he cannot sweep the grand chords of the lyre, he can j strike on golden medals his favorite maxims, and is j irreproachable in the lighter order of poetry." But, I contend, there was a fundamental earnestness in his character; he was the apostle of plain every-day common sense and good feeling.

Voltaire is judged by the character which distinguishes him from other writers, his light touch and superficial raillery. Because he is *par excellence* a *persifleur*, he is set down as merely a *persifleur*. Never was there a greater mistake. It is forgotten that he did not write witty tales and squibs only; that he made France acquainted with the philosophy of Locke and the science of Newton; that he wrote the *Age of Louis XIV.*, the *History of the Parliament of Paris*, and the *Essay on Manners* (which revived the historic method), and that he wrote more than twenty tragedies which transformed the French theatre. Voltaire was no mere mocker: his *manner* was that of a *persifleur*, but his matter was as solid as that of any theologian.

M. Louis de Brouckere, of the University of Brussels, justly claims for Voltaire a double share in the formation of modern culture and the development of modern science. He contributed to it directly by his personal works, and indirectly by antagonising the forces retarding knowledge and creating an intellectual environment eminently favorable to the formation of synthetic knowledge, and a new public opinion common to the intellectual *élite* of Europe.

Voltaire knew how to marshal against reigning prejudices and errors all the resources of vast learning and an incomparable wit; but no one more clearly than he saw that the doctrines he destroyed must be replaced by others, that humanity cannot get along without a body of common beliefs; and he contributed more than any one else to the elaboration of the new intellectual code by uniting and harmonising the efforts of special *savants* and isolated thinkers, by giving them a clear consciousness that what they aimed at was the same thing and common to them all.

He never slackened his efforts to appease the quarrels which broke out in the camp of the philosophers, to group all his *spiritual brothers* in one compact bundle, capable of joint action, to unite them in a laic *church* which could be utilised to oppose existing churches. The words I here italicise were underlined by him; they are found on every page of his correspondence, and he loses no opportunity to reiterate them and explain their meaning precisely.

If the publication of the *Encyclopædia* was the work of Diderot, the union of the group of men who rendered that publication possible was, in great measure, the work of Voltaire. If Condorcet wrote just before his death his immortal *Sketch*, Voltaire took a preponderating part in the creation of the intellectual atmosphere in which Condorcet lived and could develop his genius.

Voltaire was assuredly not so coarse as Luther, nor even as his contemporary Warburton. He carried lighter guns than Luther, but was more alert and equally persistent. His war against superstition and intolerance was life-long. Luther smote powerful blows at the church with a bludgeon; Voltaire made delicate passes with a rapier. Catholics often declaim against the coarseness of the monk-trained Protestant champion. They also protest against the trickery of the Jesuit-trained Freethinker. It is sufficient to say Luther could not have done his work had he not been coarse. Nor could Voltaire have done his had he not been a tricksy spirit. Judged by his work, he was one of the best of men, because he did most good to his fellows, and because in his heart was the most burning love of truth, of justice and toleration. In the words of Lecky, he did "more to destroy the greatest of human curses than any other of the sons of men." His numerous volumes are the fruit and exposition of a spirit of encyclopaedic curiosity. He assimilated all the thought and learning of his time, and brought to bear on it a wit and common sense that was all his own.

Voltaire is never so passionately in earnest as when he speaks against cruelty and oppression. Every sentence quivers with humanity. He denounces war as no "moralist for hire" in a pulpit has ever done, as a scourge of the poor, the weak, and the helpless, to whom he is ever tender. Whenever he sees tyranny or injustice, he attacks it. He wrote against torture when its employment was an established principle of law. He denounced duelling when that form of murder was the chief feature of the code of honor. He waged warfare upon war when, it was considered man's highest glory.

His attacks on the judicial iniquity of torture—so often callously employed on those supposed instruments of Satan, heretics and witches—were incessant, and it was owing to his influence that the practice was abolished in France by Turgot, his friend, as it had been in Prussia by Frederick, and in Russia by Catherine, his disciples. He advocated the abolition of mutilation, and all forms of cruelty in punishment. He satirised the folly of punishing murder and robbery by the same capital penalty, and thus making assassination the interest of the thief; the barbarity of confiscating the property of children for the crime of the father; and the intricacies and consequent injustice of legal methods. He sought to abolish the sale of offices, to equalise taxation, and to restrict the power of priests to prescribe degrading penances and excessive abstinences. He wrote with fervor against the remnants of serfdom, and defended the rights of the serfs in the Jura against their monastic oppressors. Mr. Lecky says: "His keen and luminous intellect judged with admirable precision most of the popular delusions of his time. He exposed with great force the common error which confounds all wealth with the precious metals. He wrote against sumptuary laws. He refuted Rousseau's doctrine of the evil of all luxury."

Voltaire's work went deeper than political reform. He dealt with ideas, not institutions. In a little treatise called the *Voyage of Reason*, which he wrote as late as 1774, he enumerates with exultation the triumphs of reforms which he himself had witnessed. He had previously written, in 1764: "Everything I see scatters the seeds of a revolution which will indubitably arrive, and which I shall not have the happiness to witness." Buckle notes that "the further he advanced in years, the more pungent were his sarcasms against ministers, the more violent were his invectives against despotism"; and it was said of him in the early days of the Revolution, when it was sanguine but not yet sanguinary, "He did not see what has been done, but he did all that we see."

He teaches no mystery, but the open secret of Secularism—*il faut cultiver nôtre jardin* (we must cultivate our garden). "Life," he said, "is thickly sown with thorns. I know no other remedy than to pass rapidly over them. The longer we dwell on our misfortunes the greater is their power to harm us." Economy, he declared, is the source of liberality, and this maxim he reduced to practice. He ridiculed all pretences; those of the physician as well as of the metaphysician. "What have you undertaken?" he said, smiling, to a young man, who answered that he was studying medicine. "Why, to convey drugs of which you know little into a body of which you know less!" "Regimen," said he, "is better than physic. Everyone should be his own physician. Eat with moderation what you know by experience agrees with your constitution. Nothing is good for the body but what we can digest. What medicine can procure digestion? Exercise. What recruit strength? Sleep. What alleviate incurable evils? Patience."

The tone of Voltaire is not fervid or heroic, like, for instance, that of Carlyle; but he worked, as Carlyle did not, for a great cause. He felt for suffering outside himself. Without mysticism or fanaticism, aiming at no remote or impracticable ideal, he ever insisted on meeting the problems of life with practical good sense, toleration, and humanity. He sought always for clear ideas, tangible results, and as Mr. Lecky says, "labored steadily within the limits of his ideals and of his sympathies, to make the world wiser, happier, and better place than he found it."

Voltaire wrote: "My motto is, 'Straight to the fact,'" and this was a characteristic which equally marked him and Frederick. He had a horror of phrases. "Your fine phrases," said one to him. "My fine phrases! Learn that I never made one in my life." His style is indeed marked by restraint and simplicity of diction. He wrote to D'Alembert: "You will never succeed in delivering men from error by means of metaphysics. You must prove the truth by facts." As an instance of his apt mingling of fact with reason and ridicule, take his treatment of the doctrine of the Resurrection in the *Philosophical Dictionary*. "A Breton soldier goes to Canada. He finds by chance he falls short of food. He is forced to eat an Iroquois he has killed over-night. This Iroquois had nourished himself on Jesuits during two or three months, a great part of his body has become Jesuit. So there is the body of this soldier composed of Iroquois, Jesuit, and whatever he had eaten before. How will each resume precisely what belonged to him?"

Magnify his failings as you may, you cannot obliterate his one transcendent merit, his humanity ever responsive to every claim of suffering or wrong. He stood for the rights of conscience, for the dignity of human reason, for the gospel of Freethought.

Voltaire may not be placed with the great inspiring teachers of mankind. But it must be acknowledged that, as Mr. George Saintsbury, no mean critic, says: "In literary craftsmanship, at once versatile and accomplished, he has no superior and scarcely a rival."

He declared that he loved the whole of the nine Muses, and that the doors of the soul should be open to all sciences and all sentiments. He employed every species of composition—poetry, prose, tragedy, comedy, history, dialogue, epistle, essay or epigram—as it suited his purpose, and he excelled in all. Argument or raillery came alike. He made reason amusing, and none like him could ridicule the ridiculous. His charm as a writer has been the occasion of the obloquy attached to his name by bigots. They can never forgive that he forced people to smile at their superstition.

Much, of course, of Voltaire's multitudinous work was directed to immediate ends, and but for his grace of style would be of little present interest. But after all winnowings by the ever-swaying fan of time much is left of enduring value. The name of Voltaire will ever be a mighty one in literature: a glorious example of what a man may achieve who is strong in his love of humanity.

TRIBUTES TO VOLTAIRE

AS a contrast to the views of Dr. Johnson and De Maistre, which for generations represented the current opinion of Protestants and Catholics, I bring together a few independent testimonies. As time goes on his admirers increase in volume, while his detractors now are mainly those who have an interest in or secret sympathy with the abuses he destroyed. And first, I will give the testimony of Goldsmith who had met him. It was written while Voltaire was alive, but when a false report of his death had been received in England. "Should you look for the character of Voltaire among the journalists and illiterate writers of the age, you will find him there characterised as a monster, with a head turned to wisdom, and a heart inclining to vice—the powers of his mind and the baseness of his principles forming a detestable contrast. But seek for his character among writers like himself, and you will find him very differently described. You perceive him, in their accounts, possessed of good nature, humanity, greatness of soul, fortitude, and almost every virtue: in this description those who might be supposed best acquainted with his character are unanimous. The royal Prussian, D'Argens, Diderot, D'Alembert, and Fontenelle conspire in drawing the picture, in describing the friend of man, and the patron of every rising genius."

Lord Byron's lines on Voltaire and Gibbon (*Childe Harold*, iii., 105-107) are well known. He says:

They were gigantic minds, and their steep aim

Was, Titan-like, on daring doubts to pile

Thoughts which should call down thunder, and the flame

Of Heaven again assail'd, if Heaven the while

On man and man's research could deign do more than smile.

The one was fire and fickleness, a child

Most mutable in wishes, but in mind

A wit as various,—gay, grave, sage, or wild,—

Historian, bard, philosopher, combined;

He multiplied himself among mankind,

The Proteus of their talents:

But his own

Breathed most in ridicule,—which, as the wind,

Blew where it listed, laying all things prone,—

Now to o'erthrow a fool, and now to shake a throne.

The other, deep and slow, exhausting thought,

And having wisdom with each studious year,

In meditation dwelt, with learning wrought,

And shaped his weapon with an edge severe,

Sapping a solemn creed with solemn sneer;

The lord of iron,—that master-spell,

Which stung his foes to wrath, which grew from fear,

And doom'd him to the zealot's ready Hell,

Which answers to all doubts so eloquently well.

Warton, the learned critic and author of a *History of Poetry* (Dissertation I.) remarked: "Voltaire, a writer of much deeper research than is imagined, and the first who has displayed the literature and customs of the dark ages with any degree of penetration and comprehension." Robertson, the historian, similarly observed that, had Voltaire only given his authorities, "many of his readers who only consider him as an entertaining and lively writer would have found that he is a learned and well informed historian."

Lord Holland wrote, in his account of the *Life and Writings of Lope de Vega*: "Till Voltaire appeared there was no nation more ignorant of its neighbors' literature than the French. He first exposed and then corrected this neglect in his countrymen. There is no writer to whom the authors of other nations, especially of England, are so indebted for the extension of their fame in France, and, through France, in Europe. There is no critic who has employed more time, wit, ingenuity, and diligence in promoting the literary intercourse between country and country, and in celebrating in one language the triumphs of another. His enemies would fain persuade us that such exuberance of wit implies a want of information; but they only succeed in showing that a want of wit by no means implies an exuberance of information."

Goethe said: "Voltaire will ever be regarded as the greatest name in literature in modern times, and perhaps even in all ages, as the most astonishing creation of nature, in which she united, in one frail human organisation, all the varieties of talent, all the glories of genius, all the potencies of thought.

If you wish depth, genius, imagination, taste, reason, sensibility, philosophy, elevation, originality, nature, intellect, fancy, rectitude, facility, flexibility, precision, art, abundance, variety, fertility, warmth, magic, charm, grace, force, an eagle sweep of vision, vast understanding, instruction rich, tone excellent, urbanity, suavity, delicacy, correctness, purity, cleanness, eloquence, harmony, brilliancy, rapidity, gaiety, pathos, sublimity and universality—perfection indeed—behold Voltaire."

Lord Brougham, in his *Lives of Men of Letters and Science who flourished in the time of George III.*, devotes a considerable section to Voltaire. After censuring "the manner in which he devoted himself to crying down the sacred things of his country," he continues: "But, though it would be exceedingly wrong to pass over this great and prevailing fault without severe reprobation, it would be equally unjust, nay, ungrateful, ever to forget the immense obligations under which Voltaire has laid mankind by his writings, the pleasure derived from his fancy and his wit, the amusement which his singular and original humor bestows, even the copious instruction with which his historical works are pregnant, and the vast improvement in the manner of writing history which we owe to him. Yet, great as these services are—among the greatest that can be rendered by a man of letters—they are really of far inferior value to the benefits which have resulted from his long and arduous struggle against oppression, especially against tyranny in the worst form which it can assume, the persecution of opinion, the infraction of the sacred right to exercise the reason upon all subjects, unfettered by prejudice, uncontrolled by authority, whether of great names or of temporal power."

Macaulay, in his *Essay on Frederick the Great*, observes: "In truth, of all the intellectual weapons which have ever been wielded by man, the most terrible was the mockery of Voltaire. Bigots and tyrants, who had never been moved by the wailing and cursing of millions, turned pale at his name."

Carlyle, in his depreciatory essay, acknowledged: "Perhaps there is no writer, not a mere compiler, but writing from his own invention or elaboration, who has left so many volumes behind him; and if to the merely arithmetical we add a critical estimate, the singularity is still greater; for these volumes are not written without an appearance of due care and preparation; perhaps there is not one altogether feeble and confused treatise, nay, one feeble and confused sentence to be found in them." And at the end he admits: "He gave the death-stab to modern Superstition! *That* horrid incubus, which dwelt in darkness, shunning the light, is passing away; with all its racks and poison chalices, and foul sleeping-draughts, is passing away without return. It was a most weighty service."

One of the strangest of tributes to Voltaire is that from Ruskin, the disciple of Carlyle. In his *Fors Clavigera* (vol. viii., p. 76) he says: "There are few stronger adversaries to St. George than Voltaire. But my scholars are welcome to read as much of Voltaire as they like. His voice is mighty among the ages."

Dr. D. F. Strauss wrote: "Voltaire's historical significance has been illustrated by the observation of Goethe that, as in families whose existence has been of long duration, Nature sometimes at length produces an individual who sums up in himself the collective qualities of all his ancestors, so it happens also with nations, whose collective merits (and demerits) sometimes appear epitomised in one individual person. Thus in Louis XIV. stood forth the highest figure of a French monarch. Thus, in Voltaire, the highest conceivable and congenial representative of French authorship. We may extend the observation farther, if, instead of the French nation only, we take into view the whole European generation on which Voltaire's influence was exercised. From this point of view we may call Voltaire emphatically the representative writer of the eighteenth century, as Goethe called him, in the highest sense, the representative writer of France."

Victor Hugo, in the magnificent oration which he pronounced on the centenary of Voltaire's death, said: "Voltaire waged the splendid kind of warfare, the war of one alone against all—that is to say, the grand warfare; the war of thought against matter; the war of reason against prejudice; the war of the just against the unjust; the war of the oppressed against the oppressor; the war of goodness; the war of kindness. He had the tenderness of a woman and the wrath of a hero. He was a great mind and an immense heart. He conquered the old code and the old dogma. He conquered the feudal lord, the Gothic judge, the Roman priest. He raised the populace to the dignity of people. He taught, pacified, and civilised. He fought for Sirven and Montbailly, as for Calas and La Barre. He accepted all the menaces, all the persecutions, calumny, and exile. He was indefatigable and immovable. He conquered violence by a smile, despotism by sarcasm, infallibility by irony, obstinacy by perseverance, ignorance by truth."

Buckle, in his *History of Civilisation* (vol. ii., p. 304) says: "It would be impossible to relate all the original remarks of Voltaire, which, when he made them, were attacked as dangerous paradoxes, and are now valued as sober truths. He was the first historian who recommended universal freedom of trade; and although he expresses himself with great caution, still, the mere announcement of the idea is a popular history forms an epoch in the progress of the French mind. He is the originator of that important distinction between the increase of population and the increase of food, to which political economy has been greatly indebted, a principle adopted several years later by Townsend, and then used by Malthus as the basis of his celebrated work. He has, moreover, the merit of being the first who dispelled the childish admiration with which the Middle Ages had been hitherto regarded.

In his works the Middle Ages are for the first time represented as what they really were—a period of ignorance, ferocity, and licentiousness; a period when injuries were unredressed, crime unpunished, and superstition unrebuked." Again (page 308): "No one reasoned more closely than Voltaire when reasoning suited his purpose. But he had to deal with men impervious to argument; men whose inordinate reverence for antiquity had only left them two ideas, namely, that everything old is right, and that everything new is wrong. To argue against these opinions would be idle indeed; the only other resource was to make them ridiculous, and weaken their influence by holding up their authors to contempt. This was one of the tasks Voltaire set himself to perform; and he did it well. He therefore used ridicule, not as the test of truth, but as the scourge of folly. And with such effect was the punishment administered that not only did the pedants and theologians of his own time wince under the lash, but even their successors feel their ears tingle when they read his biting words; and they revenge themselves by reviling the memory of the great writer whose works are as a thorn in their side, and whose very name they hold in undisguised abhorrence."

Mr. Lecky, in his *History of Rationalism in Europe* (vol. ii., p. 66) says: "Voltaire was at all times the unflinching opponent of persecution. No matter how powerful was the persecutor, no matter how insignificant was the victim, the same scathing eloquence was launched against the crime, and the indignation of Europe was soon concentrated upon the oppressor. The fearful storm of sarcasm and invective that avenged the murder of Calas, the magnificent dream in the *Philosophical Dictionary* reviewing the history of persecution from the slaughtered Canaanites to the latest victim who had perished at the stake, the indelible stigma branded upon the persecutors of every age and of every creed, all attested the intense and passionate earnestness with which Voltaire addressed himself to his task. On other subjects a jest or a caprice could often turn him aside. When attacking intolerance he employed, indeed, every weapon; but he employed them all with the concentrated energy of a profound conviction. His success was equal to his zeal; the spirit of intolerance sank blasted beneath his genius. Wherever his influence passed, the arm of the inquisitor was palsied, the chain of the captive riven, the prison door flung open. Beneath his withering irony, persecution appeared not only criminal but loathsome, and since his time it has ever shrunk from observation and masked its features under other names. He died, leaving a reputation that is indeed far from spotless, but having done more to destroy the greatest of human curses than any other of the sons of men."

Mr. Lecky, in his *History of England in the Eighteenth Century* (v., 312), observes: "No previous writer can compare with him in the wideness and justness of his conceptions of history, and even now no historian can read without profit his essays on the subject. No one before had so strongly urged that history should not be treated as a collection of pictures or anecdotes relating to courts or battles, but should be made a record and explanation of the true development of nations, of the causes of their growth and decay, of their characteristic virtues and vices, of the changes that pass over their laws, customs, opinions, social and economical conditions, and over the relative importance and well-being of their different classes... (p. 315). Untiring industry, an extraordinary variety of interests and aptitudes, a judgment at once sound, moderate, and independent, a rare power of seizing in every subject the essential argument or facts, a disposition to take no old opinions on trust and to leave no new opinions unexamined, combined in him with the most extraordinary literary talent. Never, perhaps, was there an intellect at once so luminous, versatile, and flexible, which produced so much, which could deal with such a vast range of difficult subjects without being ever obscure, tangled, or dull."

Colonel Hamley wrote: "But after the winnowings of generations, a wide and deep repute still remains to him; nor will any diminution which it may have suffered be without compensation, for, with the fading of old prejudices, and with better knowledge, his name will be regarded with increased liking and respect. Yet it must not be supposed that he is here held up as a pattern man. He was, indeed, an infinitely better one than the religious bigots of that time. He believed, with far better effect on his practice than they could boast, in a Supreme Ruler. He was the untiring and eloquent advocate at the bar of the universe of the rights of humanity."

Mr. Swinburne has well expressed this characteristic. "Voltaire's great work," he says, "was to have done more than any other man on record to make the instinct of cruelty not only detestable, but ludicrous; and so to accomplish what the holiest and the wisest of saints and philosophers had failed to achieve: to attack the most hideous and pernicious of human vices with a more effective weapon than preaching and denunciation: to make tyrants and torturers look not merely horrible and hateful, but pitiful and ridiculous."

Edgar Quinet, in his lectures on the Church, says: "I watch for forty years the reign of one man who is himself the spiritual direction, not of his country, but of his age. From the corner of his chamber he governs the realm of mind. Everyday intellects are regulated by his; one word written by his hand traverses Europe. Princes love and kings fear him. Nations repeat the words that fall from his pen. Who exercises this incredible power which has nowhere been seen since the Middle Ages? Is he another Gregory VII? Is he a Pope? No—Voltaire."

And Lamartine, in similar strain, remarks: "If we judge of men by what they have *done*, then Voltaire is incontestibly the greatest writer of modern Europe. No one has caused, through the powerful influence of his genius alone and the perseverance of his will, so great a commotion in the minds of men. His pen aroused a sleeping world, and shook a far mightier empire than that of Charlemagne, the European empire of a theocracy. His genius was not *force*, but *light*. Heaven had destined him not to destroy, but to illuminate; and wherever he trod, light followed him, for Reason—which is light—had destined him to be, first her poet, then her apostle, and lastly her idol."

Mr. Alexander A. Knox, writing in the *Nineteenth Century* (October 1882), says: "That the man's aspirations were in the main noble and honorable to humanity, I am sure. I am equally so that few men have exercised so great an influence upon their fellow creatures.... The wonderful old man! When he was past eighty years of age he set to work, like another Jeremy Bentham, to abolish the admission of hearsay evidence into French legal proceedings. But his great work was that by his wit and irony he broke down the *principle of authority* which had been so foully abused in France. Would the most strictly religious man wish to see religion as it was in France in the eighteenth century? Would the greatest stickler for authority wish to find a country governed as France was governed in the days of Voltaire?"

Du Bois-Reymond, the eminent German scientist, remarks: "Voltaire is so little to us at present because the things he fought for, 'toleration, spiritual freedom, human dignity, justice,' have become, as it were, the air we breathe, and do not think of except when we are deprived of it."

Col. R. G. Ingersoll, in his fine *Oration on Voltaire*, observes: "Voltaire was perfectly equipped for his work. A perfect master of the French language, knowing all its moods, tenses, and declinations—in fact and in feeling playing upon it as skilfully as Paganini on his violin, finding expression for every thought and fancy, writing on the most serious subjects with the gaiety of a harlequin, plucking jests from the mouth of death, graceful as the waving of willows, dealing in double meanings that covered the asp with flowers and flattery, master of satire and compliment, mingling them often in the same line, always interested himself, therefore interesting others, handling thoughts, questions, subjects as a juggler does balls, keeping them in the air with perfect ease, dressing old words in new meanings, charming, grotesque, pathetic, mingling mirth with tears, wit and wisdom, and sometimes wickedness, logic and laughter. With a woman's instinct, knowing the sensitive nerves—just where to touch—hating arrogance of place, the stupidity, of the solemn, snatching masks from priest and king, knowing the springs of action and ambition's ends, perfectly familiar with the great world, the intimate of kings and their favorites, sympathising with the oppressed and imprisoned, with the unfortunate and poor, hating tyranny, despising superstition, and loving liberty with all his heart. Such was Voltaire, writing *Œdipus* at seventeen, *Irène* at eighty-three, and crowding between these two tragedies the accomplishment of a thousand lives."

The Right Hon. John Morley testifies: "Voltaire was the very eye of modern illumination. It was he who conveyed to his generation in a multitude of forms the consciousness at once of the power and the rights of human intelligence. Another might well have said of him what he magnanimously said of his famous contemporary, Montesquieu, that humanity had lost its title-deeds, and he had recovered them. The four-score volumes which he wrote are the monument, as they were the instrument, of a new renascence. They are the fruit and representation of a spirit of encyclopaedic curiosity and productiveness. Hardly a page of all these countless leaves is common form. Hardly a sentence is there which did not come forth alive from Voltaire's own mind, or which was said because some one else had said it before. Voltaire was a stupendous power, not only because his expression was incomparably lucid, or even because his sight was exquisitely keen and clear, but because he saw many new things, after which the spirits of others were unconsciously groping and dumbly yearning. Nor was this all. Voltaire was ever in the front and centre of the fight. His life was not a mere chapter in a history of literature. He never counted truth a treasure to be discreetly hidden in a napkin. He made it a perpetual war cry, and emblazoned it on a banner that was many a time rent, but was never out of the field." We may fitly conclude with Browning's incisive lines in *The Two Poets of Croisic*:—

"Ay, sharpest, shrewdest steel that ever stabbed

To death Imposture through the armour joints."

SELECTIONS FROM VOLTAIRE'S WORKS

History

THE world is old, but history is of yesterday.—*Mélanges Historiques.*

If you would put to profit the present time, one must not spend his life in propagating ancient fables.—*Ibid.*

A mature man who has serious business does not repeat the tales of his nurse.—*Ibid.*

Search through all nations and you will not find one whose history does not begin with stories worthy of the Four Sons of Aymon and of Robert the Devil.—*Politique et Legislation.*

Ancient histories are enigmas proposed by antiquity to posterity, which understands them not—*Dict. Phil.* (Art. "Histoire").

A real fact is of more value than a hundred antitheses.—*Melanges Historiques.*

I have a droll idea. It is that only people who have written tragedies can throw interest into our dry and barbarous history. There is necessary in a history, as in a drama, exposition, knotty plot, and *dénouement*, with agreeable episode.—*Corr. gén.* 1740.

They have made but the history of the kings, not that of the nation. It seems that during fourteen hundred years there were only kings, ministers, and generals among the Gauls. But our morals, our laws, our customs, our intelligence—are these then nothing?—*Corr.*, 1740.

Is fraud sanctified by being antiquated?—*Sottisier.*

I have ever esteemed it charlatanry to paint, other than by facts, public men with whom we have had no connection.—*Corr. gen.*, 1752.

If one surveys the history of the world, one finds weaknesses punished, but great crimes fortunate, and the world is a vast scene of brigandages abandoned to fortune.—*Essai sur les Mœurs*, c. 191.

Since the ancient Romans, I have known no nation enriched by victories.—*Contant d' Orville*, i. 337.

To buy peace from an enemy is to furnish him with the sinews of war.—*Ibid*, p. 334.

The grand art of surprising, killing, and robbing is a heroism of the highest antiquity.—*Dial.* 24.

Murderers are punished, unless they kill in grand company to the sound of trumpets; that is the rule.—*Dict. Phil.* (Art. "Droit").

We formerly made war in order to eat; but in the long run, all the admirable institutions degenerate.—*Dial.* 24.

It suffices often that a mad Minister of State shall have bitten another Minister for the rabies to be communicated in a few months to five hundred thousand men.—*Ibid.*

In this world there (are) only offensive wars; defensive ones are only resistance to armed robbers.—*Ibid.*

Twenty volumes in folio never yet made a revolution. It is the portable little shilling books that are to be feared. If the Gospel cost twelve hundred sesterces, the Christian religion would never have been established.—*Correspondence with D1 Alembert*, 1765.

Wars

C.: What, you do not admit there are just wars?

A.: I have never known any of the kind; to me it appears contradictory and impossible.

C.: What! when the Pope Alexander VI. and his infamous son Borgia pillaged the Roman States, strangled and poisoned the lords of the land, while according them indulgences: was it not permissible to arm against these monsters?

A.: Do you not see that it was these monsters who made war? Those who defended themselves from aggression but sustained it. There are constantly only offensive wars in this world; the defensive is nothing but resistance to armed robbers.

C.: You mock us. Two princes dispute an heritage, their right is litigious, their reasons equally plausible; it is necessary then that war should decide, and this war is just on both sides.

A.: It is you who mock. It is physically impossible that both are right, and it is absurd and barbarous that the people should perish because one of these two princes has reasoned badly. Let them fight together in a closed field if they wish, but that an entire people should be sacrificed to their interests, there is the horror.—*l' A.B.C.*

Politics

THEY have discovered in their fine politics the art of causing those to die of hunger who, by cultivating the earth, give the means of life to others.—*Sottisier.*

Society has been too long like a game of cards, where the rogues cheat the dupes, while sensible people dare not warn the losers that they are deceived.—*Questions sur les Miracles.*

They have only inculcated belief in absurdities to men in order to subdue them.—*Ibid.*

The most tolerable of all governments is doubtless the republican, since that approaches the nearest towards natural equality.—*Idées Républicaines.*

A Republican is ever more attached to his country than a subject to his, for the same reason that one loves better his own possessions than those of a master.—*Pensées sur le Gouvernement.*

Give too much power to anybody and be sure they will abuse it. Were the monks of La Trappe spread throughout the world, let them confess princesses, educate youth, preach and write, and in about ten years they would be similar to the Jesuits, and it would be necessary to repress them.—*Mél. Balance Egale.*

What are politics beyond the art of lying a propos?—*Contant D'Orville.*

"Reasons of State" is a phrase invented to serve as excuse for tyrants.—*Commentaire sur le traité des Délits.*

The best government is that where there are the fewest useless men.—*Dial. 4.*

Man is born free. The best government is that which most preserves to each mortal this gift of nature.—*Histoire de Russie.*

To be free, to have only equals, is the true life, the natural life of man; all other is an unworthy artifice, a poor comedy, where one plays the rôle of master, the other of slave, this one a parasite, and that other a pander.—*Dial. 24.*

Why is liberty so rare? Because it is the best possession.—*Dict. Phil.* ("Venise").

Those who say that all men are equal, say truth if they mean that men have an equal right to liberty, to the property of their own goods, and the protection of the laws. They are much deceived if they think that men should be equal in their employments, since they are not so by their faculties.—*Essai sur les Mœurs*, i.

Despotism is the punishment of the bad conduct of men. If a community is mastered by one man or by several, it is plainly because it has not the courage and ability necessary for self-government.—*Idées Republic-aines*, 1765.

I do not give myself up to my fellow-citizens without reserve. I do not give them the power to kill or to rob me by plurality of votes. I submit to help them, and to be aided, to do justice, and to receive it. No other agreement.—*Notes on Rousseau's "Social Contract"*

The Population Question

The Man of Forty Crowns: I have heard much talk of population. Were we to take it into our heads to beget double the number of children we now do; were our country doubly peopled, so that we had forty millions of inhabitants instead of twenty, what would happen?

The Geometrician: Each would have, instead of forty, but twenty crowns to live upon; or the land would have to produce the double of what it now does; or there would be the double of the nation's industry, or of gain from foreign countries; or one half of the nation sent to America; or the one half of the nation should eat the other.—*The Man of Forty Crowns.*

Nature's Way

NATURE cares very little for individuals. There are other insects which do not live above one day, but of which the species is perpetual. Nature resembles those great princes who reckon as nothing the loss of four hundred thousand men, so they but accomplish their august designs.— *The Man of Forty Crowns.*

Prayer

WHEN the man of forty crowns saw himself the father of a son, he began to think himself a man of some weight in the state; he hoped to furnish, at least, ten subjects to the king, who should all prove useful. He made the best baskets in the world, and his wife was an excellent sempstress. She was born in the neighborhood of a rich abbey of a hundred thousand livres a year. Her husband asked me, one day, why those gentlemen, who were so few in number, had swallowed so many of the forty crown lots? "Are they more useful to their country than I am?"—"No, dear neighbor."—"Do they, like me, contribute at least to the population of it?"—"No, not to appearance, at least."—"Do they cultivate the land? Do they defend the state when it is attacked?"—"No, they pray to God for us."—"Well, then, I will pray to God for them, and let us go snacks."—*The Man of Forty Crowns.*

Doubt and Speculation

The Man of Forty Crowns: I have sometimes a great mind to laugh at all I have been told.

The Geometrician: And a very good mind it is. I advise you to doubt of everything, except that the three angles of a triangle are equal to two right ones, and that triangles which have the same bases and height are equal to one another; or like propositions, as, for example, that two and two make four.

The Man of Forty Crowns: Yes; I hold it very wise to doubt; but I am curious since I have made my fortune and have leisure. I could wish, when my will moves my arm or my leg, to discover the spring, for surely there is one, by which my will moves them. I wonder sometimes why I can lift or lower my eyes, yet cannot move my ears. I think—and I wish I could know a little how—I mean,—there, to have my thought palpable to me, to touch it, as it were. That would surely be very curious. I want to find out whether I think from myself, or whether it is God that gives me my ideas; whether my soul came into my body at six weeks, or at one day old; how it lodged itself in my brain; whether I think much when in a profound sleep, or in a lethargy. I torture my brains to know how one body impels another. My sensations are no less a wonder to me; I find something divine in them, and especially in pleasure. I have striven sometimes to imagine a new sense, but could never arrive at it. Geometricians know all these things; kindly be so good as to teach me.

The Geometrician: Alas! We are as ignorant as you. Apply to the Sorbonne.

Dr. Pangloss and the Dervish

IN the neighborhood lived a very famous dervish, who was deemed the best philosopher in Turkey; him they went to consult. Pangloss was spokesman and addressed him thus:—

"Master, we come to beg you to tell us why so strange an animal as man has been formed?"

"Why do you trouble your head about it?" said the dervish; "is it any business of yours?"

"But, reverend father," said Candide, "there is a horrible amount of evil on the earth."

"What signifies it," says the dervish, "whether there is evil or good? When His Highness sends a ship to Egypt does he trouble whether the rats aboard are comfortable or not?"

"What is to be done, then?" says Pangloss.

"Be silent," answers the dervish.

"I flattered myself," replied Pangloss, "to have reasoned a little with you on causes and effects, the best of possible worlds, the origin of evil, the nature of the soul, and on pre-established harmony."

At these words the dervish shut the door in their faces.—*Candide*.

Motives for Conduct

Countess: Apropos, I have forgotten to ask your opinion upon a matter which I read yesterday in a story by these good Mohammedans, which much struck me. Hassan, son of Ali, being bathing, one of his slaves threw over him by accident some boiling water. His servants wished to impale the culprit. Hassan, instead, gave him twenty pieces of gold. "There is," said he, "a degree of glory in Paradise for those who repay services, a greater one for those who forgive evil, and a still greater one for those who recompense involuntary evil." What think you of his action and his speech?

The Count: I recognise there my good Moslems of the first ages.

Abbé: And I, my good Christians.

M. Fréret: And I am sorry that the scalded Hassan, son of Ali, should have given twenty pieces of gold in order to have glory in Paradise. I do not like interested fine actions. I should have wished that Hassan had been sufficiently virtuous and humane to have consoled the despair of the slave without even dreaming of being placed in the third rank in Paradise.—*Le Diner du Comte de Boulainvilliers*.

Self-Love

SELF-love and all its off-shoots are as necessary to man as the blood which flows in his veins. Those who would take away his passions because they are dangerous resemble those who would deplete a man of all his blood lest he should fall into apoplexy.—*Traité de Metaphysique*.

Go From Your Village

A STUPID said: "I must think like my *bonze* (priest), for all my village agrees with him." Go from your village, poor man, and you will find ten thousand others who have each their *bonze*, and who all think differently.

Religious Prejudices

IF your nurse has told you that Ceres presides over corn, or that Vishnu or Sakyamuni became men several times, or that Odin awaits you in his hall towards Jutland, or that Mohammed or some other travelled to Heaven; if, moreover, your preceptor deepens in your brain what the nurse, has engraved, you will hold it all your life. Should your judgment rise against these prejudices, your neighbors, above all your female neighbors, will cry out at the impiety and frighten you. Your dervish, fearing the diminution of his revenue, may accuse you before the Cadi, and this Cadi impale you if he can, since he desires to rule over fools, believing fools obey better than others; and this will endure till your neighbors, and the dervish, and the Cadi begin to understand that folly is good for nothing and that persecution is abominable.—*Dictionnaire Philosophique.*

Sacred History

I ABANDON to the declaimer Bossuet the politics of the Kings of Judah and Samaria, who only understood assassination, beginning with their King David (who took to the trade of brigand to make himself king, and assassinated Uriah when he was his master); and to wise Solomon, who began by assassinating Adonijah, his own brother, at the foot of the altar. I am tired of the absurd pedantry which consecrates the history of such a people to the instruction of children.—*l'A.B.C.*

Dupe And Rogue

ARE there theologians of good faith? Yes, as there have been men who believed themselves sorcerers.—*Le Diner du Comte de Boulainvilliers.*

Enthusiasm begins, roguery ends. It is with religion as with gambling. One begins by being dupe, one ends by being rogue.—*Le Diner du Comte de Boulainvilliers.*

Every country has its bonzes. But I recognise that there are as many of them deceived as deceivers. The majority are those blinded by enthusiasm in their youth, and who never recover sight; there are others who have preserved one eye, and see all squintingly. These are the stupid charlatans.—*Entre deux Chinois.*

"Delenda Est Carthago"

THEOLOGY must absolutely be destroyed, just as judicial astrology, magic, the divining rod, and the Star Chamber have been destroyed.—*l'A.B.C.*

Jesus and Mohammed

L'Abbé: How could Christianity have established itself so high if it had nothing but fanaticism and fraud at its base?

Le Comte: And how did Mohammedanism establish itself. Mohammed at least could write and fight, and Jesus knew neither writing nor self-defence. Mohammed had the courage of Alexander, with the mind of Numa; and your Jesus, sweat, blood, and water. Mohammedanism has never changed, while you have changed your religion twenty times. There is more difference between it, as it is to-day, from what it was in the first ages, than there is between your customs and those of King Dagobert.—*Le Diner du Comte de Boulainvilliers.*

How Faiths Spread

BUT how do you think, then, that my religion became established? Like all the rest. A man of strong imagination made himself followed by some persons of weak imagination. The flock increased; fanaticism commences, fraud achieves. A powerful man comes; he sees a crowd, ready bridled and with a bit in its teeth; he mounts and leads it.—*Dial, et entr. ph., Dialogue 19.*

Superstition

THE superstitious man is to the knave what the slave is to the tyrant; nay, further, the superstitious man is governed by the fanatic, and becomes one.—*Dict. Phil. (Art. "Superstition").*

The Bible

IF there are many difficulties we cannot solve, mysteries we cannot comprehend, adventures which we cannot credit, prodigies which display the credulity of the human mind, and contradictions which it is impossible to reconcile, it is in order to exercise our faith and to-humiliate our reason.—*Dict. Phil.* (Art. "Contradictions").

Transubstantiation

JULIUS II. makes and eats God; but with armor on his back and helmet on his head he wades in blood and carnage. Leo X. holds God in his body, his mistresses in his arms, and the money extorted by the sale of indulgences in his coffers, and those of his sister.—*Dict. Phil.* (Art. "Eucharist").

Dreams and Ghosts

HAVE you not found, like me, that they are the origin of the opinion so generally diffused throughout antiquity touching spectres and manes? A man deeply afflicted at the death of his wife, or his son, sees them in his sleep; they have the same characteristics; he speaks to them, they reply; they have certainly appeared to him. Other men have had similar dreams. It is impossible, then, to doubt that the dead return; but it is certain at the same time that these dead—whether buried or reduced to ashes, or lost at sea— could not reappear in their bodies. It is, then, their soul that has been seen. This soul must be extended, light, impalpable, since in speaking with it we cannot embrace it. *Effugit imago per levibus vetitis* (Virgil). It is moulded, designed upon the body which it habited, since it perfectly resembles it. It is given the name of shade or manes, and from all this a confused idea remains in the head, which perpetuates itself all the better because nobody understands it.—*Dict. Phil.* (Art. "Somnambulists and Dreams").

Mortifying the Flesh

HAD vanity never any share in the public mortifications which attended the eyes of the multitude? "I scourge myself, but 'tis to expiate your faults; I go stark naked, but 'tis to reproach the luxury of your garments; I feed on herbs and snails to correct your vice of gluttony; I put an iron ring on my body to make you blush at your lewdness. Reverence me as a man cherished by the gods, who can draw down their favors on you. When accustomed to reverence, it will not be hard to obey me; I become your master in the name of the gods; and if you transgress my will in the least particular, I will have you impaled to appease the wrath of heaven." If the first fakirs did not use these words, they probably had them engraven at the bottom of their hearts.—*Dict. Phil.* (Art. "Austerities").

Heaven

Kon.: What is meant by "the heaven and the earth: mount up to heaven, be worthy of heaven"?

Cu Su.: 'Tis but stupidity, there is no heaven; each planet is surrounded by its atmosphere, and rolls in space around its sun. Each sun is the centre of several planets which travel continually around it. There is no up nor down, ascension nor descent. You perceive that if the inhabitants of the moon said that some one ascended to the earth, that one must render himself worthy of earth, he would talk nonsense. We do so likewise when we say we must be worthy of heaven; it is as if we said we must be worthy of air, worthy of the constellation of the Dragon, worthy of space.—*Catéchisme chinois*.

Magic

ALL the fathers of the Church, without exception, believed in the power of magic. The Church always condemned magic, but she always believed it; she excommunicated sorcerers, not as deluded madmen, but as men who really had intercourse with devils.—*Dict. Phil.* (Art. "Superstition").

DETACHED THOUGHTS

THERE are vices which it is better to ignore than to punish.

One should not pronounce a word in public which an honest woman cannot repeat.

I know no great men but those who have rendered great services to humanity.

Honor has ever achieved greater things than interest.

Occupation and work are the only resources against misfortune.

My maxim is to fulfil all my duties to-day, because I am not sure of living to-morrow.

Most men die before having lived.

It is necessary to combat nature and fortune till the last moment, and to never despair till one is dead.

Work without disputing; it is the only way to render life supportable.

Passions are the winds that swell the sails of the ship. It is true, they sometimes sink her, but without them she could not sail at all. The bile makes us sick and choleric; but without the bile we could not live. Everything in this world is dangerous, and yet everything in it is necessary.

We should introduce into our existence all imaginable modes, and open every door of the minds to all kinds of knowledge, and all sorts of feelings. So long as it does not all go in pell-mell, there is room enough for all.

It is the part of a man like you [Vauvenargues] to have preferences, but no exclusions.

The unwise value every word in an author of repute.

Opinion governs the world, and philosophers in the long run govern opinion.

We enjoin mankind to conquer their passions. Make the experiment of only depriving a man, in the habit of taking it, of his pinch of snuff.

Do we not nearly all resemble the aged General of ninety years, who, seeing some young fellows larking with the girls, said to them angrily: "Gentlemen, is that the example which I give you?"

Passions are diseases. To cure a man of a criminal intention, we should give him not counsel, but a dose of physic.

Women are like windmills, fixed while they revolve.

I fear lest marriage may not rather be one of the seven deadly sins than one of the seven sacraments.

Divorce is probably of about the same date as marriage.

I believe, however, that marriage is several weeks the elder.

War is an epitome of all wickedness.

The race of preachers inveigh against little vices, and pass over great ones in silence. They never sermonise against war.

What strange rage possesses some people to insist on our all being miserable? They are like a quack, who would fain have us believe we are ill, in order to sell us his pills. Keep thy drugs, my friend, and leave me my health.

Can one change their character? Yes, if one changes their body.

Men are fools, but ecclesiastics are their leaders.

I do not believe even eye-witnesses when they tell me things opposed to common sense.

The fanatics begin with humility and kindness, and have all ended with pride and carnage.

The Pope is an idol, whose hands are tied and whose feet are kissed.

What an immense book might be composed on all the things once believed, of which it is necessary to doubt.

That which can be explained in many ways does not merit being explained in any.

Theology is in religion what poison is among food.

Theology has only served to upset brains, and sometimes States.

That which is an eternal subject of dispute is an eternal inutility.

To pray is to flatter oneself that one will change entire nature with words.

Names of sects; names of error. Truth has no sect.

No man is called an Euclidian.

Henry IV., after his victories, his abjuration, and his coronation, caused a cross to be erected in Rome, with the following inscription: *In hoc signa vincis*. The wood of the cross was the carriage of a cannon.

A revolution has been accomplished in the human mind which nothing again can ever arrest.

It is never by metaphysics that you will succeed in delivering men from error; you must prove the truth by facts.

If fortune brings to pass one of a hundred events predicted by roguery, all the others are forgotten, and that one remains as a pledge of the favor of God, and as the proof of a prodigy.

Every one is born with a nose and five fingers, and no one is born with a knowledge of God. This may be deplorable or not, but it is certainly the human condition.

If God made us in his own image, we have well returned him the compliment.

Nature preserves the species, and cares but very little for individuals.

To fast, to pray, a priest's virtue; to succor, virtue of a citizen.

When Bellerophon, mounted on Pegasus, wished to ascend to heaven to discover the secrets of the gods, a fly stung Pegasus, and he was thrown.

"Why do you receive so many fools in your order?" was said to a Jesuit. "We need saints."

Rousseau [J. B.] having shown his antagonist [Voltaire] his *Ode to Posterity*, the latter said: "My friend, here is a letter which will never reach its address."

If a tulip could speak, and said, "My vegetation and I are two distinct beings, evidently joined together," would you not mock at the tulip?

Why all these pleasantries on religion? They are never made on morality.

A fanatic of good faith, always a dangerous kind of man.

The consolation of life is to say out what one thinks.